Fran and Frederick
HAMERSTROM

Other Badger Biographies

Belle and Bob La Follette: Partners in Politics

Blue Jenkins: Working for Workers

Caroline Quarlls and the Underground Railroad

Casper Jaggi: Master Swiss Cheese Maker

Cindy Bentley: Spirit of a Champion

Cordelia Harvey: Civil War Angel

Cris Plata: From Fields to Stage/Del Campo al Escenario

Curly Lambeau: Building the Green Bay Packers

Dr. Kate: Angel on Snowshoes

Electa Quinney: Stockbridge Teacher

Father Groppi: Marching for Civil Rights

Gaylord Nelson: Champion for Our Earth

Harley and the Davidsons: Motorcycle Legends

John Nelligan: Wisconsin Lumberjack

Joyce Westerman: Baseball Hero

Juliette Kinzie: Frontier Storyteller

Les Paul: Guitar Wizard

Lucius Fairchild: Civil War Hero

Mai Ya's Long Journey

Mary Nohl: A Lifetime in Art

Mountain Wolf Woman: A Ho-Chunk Girlhood

Ole Evinrude and His Outboard Motor

A Recipe for Success: Lizzie Kander and Her Cookbook

Richard Bong: World War II Flying Ace

Sterling North and the Story of Rascal

Tents, Tigers, and the Ringling Brothers

Fran and Frederick
HAMERSTROM

Wildlife Conservation Pioneers

SUSAN TUPPER

Wisconsin Historical Society Press

Published by the Wisconsin Historical Society Press
Publishers since 1855

wisconsin**history**.org

Photographs identified with WHi or WHS are from the Society's collections; address requests to reproduce these photos to the Visual Materials Archivist at the Wisconsin Historical Society, 816 State Street, Madison, WI 53706.

Front cover photo by Hans Pigorsch; back cover painting by Elva Hamerstrom Paulson.

Pen-and-ink drawings on pages 9, 29, 60, 68, and 104 are used with permission from the artist, Elva Hamerstrom Paulson.

Printed in Wisconsin, U.S.A.
Designed by Jill Bremigan

20 19 18 17 16   1 2 3 4 5

Library of Congress Cataloging-in-Publication Data

Names: Tupper, Susan.
Title: Fran and Frederick Hamerstrom : wildlife conservation pioneers / Susan
  Tupper.
Description: Madison, WI : Wisconsin Historical Society Press, 2016. |
  Series: Badger biographies | Audience: Grades 4 to 6. | Includes index.
Identifiers: LCCN 2015026161 | ISBN 9780870207327 (paperback : alkaline paper)
  | ISBN 9780870207334 (e-book)
Subjects: LCSH: Hamerstrom, Frances, 1907-1998—Juvenile literature. |
  Hamerstrom, Frederick—Juvenile literature. | Wildlife
  conservationists—Wisconsin—Biography—Juvenile literature. | Wildlife
  conservation—Wisconsin—History—20th century—Juvenile literature. |
  Endangered species—Wisconsin—History—20th century—Juvenile literature.
  | Prairie chickens—Conservation—Wisconsin—History—20th
  century—Juvenile literature. | Wisconsin—Environmental
  conditions—History—20th century—Juvenile literature. |
  Wisconsin—Biography—Juvenile literature.
Classification: LCC QL84.22.W6 T86 2016 | DDC 333.9516092/2775—dc23 LC record available
at http://lccn.loc.gov/2015026161

To my sons Devin and Ethan
To my grandson Henry
And to the future of all of our children

Contents

1 Meet Fran and Frederick Hamerstrom 1

2 Kestrels and Pollywogs 6

3 Hammy 16

4 Bug Woman and Bird Man 21

5 Welcome to Wisconsin .31

6 The Wildest of Wild Creatures 46

7 Family Life and the War Years 57

8 Boomers in the Spring .65

9 The Battle for the Chickens 75

10 Raptor Love 83

11 Those Who Capture the Doves 94

    Appendix: Fran and Frederick's Time Line 105

    Glossary 108

    Reading Group Guide and Activities 115

    To Learn More about Prairie Chickens and Other
    Endangered Species 117

    Acknowledgments 118

    Index 120

1

Meet Fran and Frederick Hamerstrom

Together, we made the decision to burn our bridges behind us and take to a life as biologists in the wilderness.

—Fran Hamerstrom

In early spring, the Buena Vista Grasslands in central Wisconsin is full of birds on the move. Many **species** of birds come to the **marsh** to nest and raise a family. Geese, cranes, and hawks fly overhead. And prairie chickens roam the grasslands, each one looking for a matc.

Every year, students from all over Wisconsin come to the marsh to count the prairie chickens. The students have been coming here for more than 70 years. They watch the prairie chickens dance. And they listen to the sound of the prairie chickens' booming call.

species (**spee** seez): a group of similar plants or animals   marsh: an area of soft wet land with grasses and related plants

PHOTO COURTESY OF DALE PAULSON

The booming call is the male prairie chicken's mating song. In the early spring dawn, the males boom to attract the attention of the females. Their booming call makes a deep, haunting

This male prairie chicken's neck feathers, called **pinnae**, are raised over his head to attract the female birds.

sound like that of a **tympani** drum in an orchestra. Some people describe the booming call as one of the most fantastic sounds in the natural world.

A long time ago, thousands of prairie chickens lived in Wisconsin. But as cities grew, the prairie chickens lost their nesting grounds. By 1850, the prairie chicken population began to decrease. In the 1950s, only about 2,500 prairie chickens still lived in Wisconsin. But 2 scientists helped to save them. Those scientists were Frances "Fran" and Frederick Hamerstrom.

tympani (**tim** puh nee): one of a set of 2 or 3 large drums that are played by one performer in an orchestra
pinnae: pin ı

WHI IMAGE ID 2290

Aldo Leopold

Fran and Frederick both grew up with a passion for wildlife. In the 1930s, Fran and Frederick were students of a famous scientist named Aldo Leopold, who was known as the "father of **ecology**."

Ecologists study plants and animals in their natural settings. They try to understand how plants and animals depend on each other. They study animals to learn why they live in one place but not another. Scientists call the places where animals live their **habitat**. All animals need a certain kind of habitat to survive. Their habitat provides the food they like to eat and the surroundings they need to nest and raise their babies.

Fran and Frederick became ecologists when ecology was a brand-new science. They learned that if habitat is disturbed,

ecology (ee **kah** luh jee): a branch of science concerned with the relationships between living things and their environment   **habitat**: the place where a plant or animal grows or lives in nature

plants die and animals either move to another place or die out. Fran and Frederick discovered that the prairie chicken's habitat was being threatened. To save the prairie chicken from **extinction**, the Hamerstroms studied the bird's habitat for more than 30 years.

PHOTO COURTESY OF DALE PAULSON

Prairie chickens on the booming grounds

Think of your favorite bird. Is it an eagle, an owl, or maybe a loon? How do you feel when you see it soaring overhead or hear its call? Now think of how much you would miss that bird if it disappeared.

extinction (ek **sting** shuhn): no longer existing or being alive

4

Fran and Frederick did not want to lose any part of our natural world. They worked hard to save plants and animals so that those plants and animals would always be here to enjoy.

Because of Fran and Frederick Hamerstrom's hard work, the prairie chickens still boom every spring on the Buena Vista Grasslands. This is the story of 2 remarkable scientists who devoted their lives to saving the prairie chickens of Wisconsin.

2

Kestrels and Pollywogs

───────────── 🐾 ─────────────

I cannot explain my passion for the wild and free.

—Fran Hamerstrom

On a cold morning in Boston in December 1907, a little girl was born to Helen and Laurence Flint. Her parents named her Frances, but she liked to be called Fran.

Young Fran loved nature and wild animals. But her family did not understand her interest in wild creatures.

Years later, when Fran was an adult, she wrote: "When I was a small child, I longed one day to become so famous that I did not have to hide how odd I was, how unlike other people. Few people really held my attention. It was birds and

Eight-year-old Fran wears one of the smocked dresses she hated.

6

mammals, reptiles, and insects that filled my dreams and eternally **whetted** my curiosity."

Young Fran in Germany

In the early 1900s, girls from wealthy families like Fran's were expected to grow up and marry rich men. Girls were taught to be good wives for their future husbands. Fran was taught to walk and sit gracefully, dance beautifully, and manage a large household.

Fran's mother dressed her in pastel pink and blue dresses from London. Fran hated the dresses. She preferred hockey sticks. Today, we are lucky that girls are encouraged to do anything they want. Can you think of some activities girls do today that might not have been allowed when Fran was little?

whetted (**hwet** id): made stronger

When Fran was 5 years old, her family moved to Germany, where her father worked as a **criminologist**. The family hired a strict German **governess** to teach Fran and her brother, Bertram. Fran had a gift for learning languages and easily learned to speak German and French. Her time in Germany left a **vivid** impression on Fran. Many years later Fran's ability to speak German would help her work with German scientists.

Two years after the family moved to Germany, World War I began. Fran's father decided it was time to return to the United States. Fran's German governess, **Frauta**, moved with them and taught her for 12 more years. Frauta's teachings influenced Fran throughout her life.

Back home in Massachusetts, Fran discovered many new delights. Her family's house was surrounded by green meadows, woods, and the wild **Neponset** River. Fran was happiest when she escaped the house and went exploring outside.

---

criminologist (krim uh **nah** luh jist): someone who studies crime, criminals, and the punishment of criminals
governess: a woman who teaches and trains a child especially in a private home   **vivid** (**vi** vuhd): very strong or bright   **Frauta**: frou **tuh**   **Neponset**: nee **pahn** set

ELVA HAMERSTROM PAULSON

An illustration of Fran's childhood home in Milton, Massachusetts

She loved to climb trees because she could get closer to the birds and observe them. She found holes in some of the trees. The holes were the perfect place to hide things she didn't want her parents to find, like knives. Knives were very valuable to Fran. She used them to cut up dead animals and birds so she could examine their organs.

Fran's mother had a beautiful flower garden. Fran spent hours in the garden, digging up fascinating beetles and worms. But one day, the family's maid was horrified to see Fran digging in broad daylight. It was unladylike. So Fran made a secret garden in a wild area behind the horse stables.

Fran planted poison ivy on the path to her secret garden to keep her family away. Fran was not allergic to poison ivy, but almost everyone else in her family was. This simple trick gave Fran a place of her own where she could keep her wild pets. She brought injured snakes, squirrels, turtles, birds, and mice to the garden and called it her "wild animal hospital."

At night, Fran climbed out of her bedroom window to sleep under a big spruce tree in the yard. Nighttime noises didn't frighten her. The frogs' croaking chorus **lulled** her to sleep. In the morning, she woke up in time to crawl back into her bed before she was discovered. Her parents never knew about her escapes into the yard at night.

No wonder Fran felt her childhood was difficult. The things she loved most had to be kept a secret from her family. Otherwise they might be taken away. Imagine how lonely and different she felt.

lulled: made sleepy

One day, after a dentist appointment, Frauta took Fran to the nearby Boston Natural History Museum. The insect collection at the museum fascinated Fran. She noticed the way all the insects were carefully mounted and labeled.

Fran longed to return to the museum, but she knew Frauta would not take her without a reason. So Fran stuck a pencil into her gums until they bled. Frauta took her back to the dentist and agreed to take her to the museum afterward. When Fran got home, she started her own insect collection.

Fran's parents, Laurence and Helen Flint

When Fran was almost 9 years old, her family spent a vacation on a nearby island called **Martha's Vineyard**. One

Martha's Vineyard: **mahr** thuhz **vin** yurd

11

WHI IMAGE ID 59194

The insect and butterfly collections shown here might be similar to the ones Fran loved as a girl.

day when she was playing with friends, a huge fire broke out on a nearby heath hen preserve. Heath hens were a species of prairie chickens that lived on the East Coast. A fire truck roared up, and a man yelled, "We need help fighting this fire!" But no one volunteered.

Later, Fran learned that all the heath hen eggs hatched that year were lost in the fire. The heath hen population dropped from around 2,000 hens to only 200 hens. They never

12

recovered. Sixteen years later, in 1932, heath hens became extinct. Many years later, Fran remembered the heath hens and said, "I learned so young about the **impending** doom of a species."

On a snowy day in late autumn when Fran was 12, a family friend gave her a pet that changed her life. The pet was a bird called a **kestrel**. From the moment Fran looked into the bird's face, she was hooked. She went straight to the public library to learn how to care for it. She discovered that the kestrel was the smallest member of the falcon family. Fran didn't tell anyone else in her family about her new pet.

Kestrels

In order to train her kestrel, Fran needed 2 **jesses**, or straps of leather used to tie the bird's legs to a leash. She remembered that her mother had several pairs of white leather gloves that she wore to the opera. One night, when her mother was gone, Fran stole a pair of gloves and cut them up to make the jesses.

impending (im **pen** ding): happening or likely to happen soon   **kestrel** (kes truhl): small falcon that hovers in the air while searching for prey   **jesses**: short straps secured on the leg of a bird, usually with a ring for attaching a leash

Fran secretly took meat from the kitchen to feed her kestrel and trained it to eat out of her hand. She also trained it to land on her hand when she whistled and to ride on her head. Caring for her kestrel inspired Fran's lifelong interest in **raptors**.

As she grew older, Fran became more **rebellious**. Once, when guests came to dinner, Fran and her brother put **pollywogs** into a pitcher of their drinking water. At night, she sometimes climbed down a tree outside her bedroom window and met friends outside. Some nights they secretly borrowed cars from their friends and families for their adventures. A few times they even broke windows and stole street lanterns. This was very dangerous, because lanterns were the only light source at night to guide people safely as they walked and drove.

When Fran was about 17 years old, she was arrested and sent to court. The judge explained that her bad behavior could hurt other people. He told Fran, "Without lanterns, someone could get killed or crippled for life."

The judge's words made sense to her. Fran began to be more considerate of others. Later, she wrote, "I hope other

raptors: birds that kill and eat other animals for food   rebellious (ruh **bel** yuhs): fighting against or refusing to obey authority   pollywog (**pah** lee wahg): a tadpole, or the larva of a frog or toad that has a long tail, breathes with gills, and lives in water

14

teenagers who feel alone and desperate as I once did, will take hope, because I eventually did turn out all right as a person, a wildlife biologist, wife, and writer."

Fran's wild ways also caused problems at school. Though she was very smart, she didn't like school. She never graduated from high school. Still, she managed to be admitted to Smith College in Massachusetts. But she flunked out during her sophomore year. She later said, "I simply didn't go to classes that bored me."

Fran needed a job. So she went to a fashionable dress shop in Boston. Though she had no experience, she convinced the owner to hire her as a model. She began thinking of a career in acting. But instead Fran fell in love.

Fran worked as a fashion model before becoming a scientist.

15

3
Hammy

We Norwegians like to think things over.

—Frederick Hamerstrom

Frederick Hamerstrom Jr. was born on July 8, 1909, in Trenton, New Jersey. In the Hamerstrom family, the tradition was to nickname the oldest boy Hammy. Frederick's closest friends called him Hammy throughout his life.

Frederick's childhood was much happier than Fran's. His father was a financial manager for several large companies. He was known for saving companies that were in debt. The family lived

Frederick as a young boy

in beautiful homes and spent vacations at the seashore. Both of Frederick's parents were gentle and loving.

Frederick's father, Frederick Hamerstrom Sr.

Frederick was a quiet, shy, and well-behaved boy. He and his younger brother, Davis, constantly played outdoors together. They spent many happy hours skating, swimming, fishing, exploring caves, and catching snakes and other wildlife. When Frederick was not outdoors, he loved to curl up in a favorite chair and read. Another favorite family activity was making ice cream on Sunday afternoons in the summer. In high school, Frederick was popular with girls because he was a good dancer. He loved

Frederick's mother, Helen Davis Hamerstrom, in her wedding photo

music and even built his own radio so he could listen to music in his bedroom.

During Frederick's high school years, his father had a harder time finding work. Frederick knew that if he wanted to go to college, he would have to work to pay for it.

Frederick found many different ways to make money. His father had a beautiful shotgun that Frederick sometimes took hunting. He became an expert shot and learned to skin the animals so he could sell the pelts. One summer, he worked as a camp counselor. Another summer he worked on a farm where he mixed and poured cement and learned other practical skills. Frederick's **reputation** for honesty and hard work stayed with him throughout his life.

Unlike Fran, Frederick studied hard in high school. When it was time to think about college, his good grades earned him a place at **Dartmouth** College in New Hampshire. Just as in high school, he picked up all kinds of odd jobs to help with college expenses. He worked at a local coffee shop and earned 40 cents an hour. He even collected and delivered laundry.

reputation (rep yoo **tay** shuhn): overall quality or character as judged by people in general
Dartmouth: dahrt muhth

HAMERSTROM FAMILY ARCHIVES

Frederick, during his time in college

In college, Frederick went to class in the morning and worked in the evening. In the afternoon, he studied and then spent time wandering through the countryside around Dartmouth. He roamed along the bluffs and the river and tried his hand at fishing. When Frederick was a freshman, the river flooded. Frederick and other students helped with the cleanup. Exploring and protecting nature was important to him.

One of Frederick's biggest influences was his uncle Clarence Darrow, who was married to his Aunt Ruby. Uncle Clarence had encouraged Frederick to go to Dartmouth. He

19

had convinced Frederick's father to let Frederick stay in college when his father was running short of money.

Uncle Clarence was one of the most famous lawyers in the United States. He had a reputation for defending poor, black, and working people. He believed the criminal system in the United States favored the rich over the poor. He fought against the use of **capital punishment** and child labor. Perhaps Uncle Clarence's desire to help the **underdog** rubbed off on his nephew. Frederick also spent his life battling for his beliefs.

The famous lawyer Clarence Darrow was married to Frederick's Aunt Ruby.

Later in life, after Frederick and Fran had met and married and moved to Wisconsin, they often visited Uncle Clarence and Aunt Ruby at their home in Chicago. Of all of Fran and Frederick's relatives, Clarence and Ruby Darrow seemed to understand Fran and Frederick the best.

capital punishment: the legally authorized killing of someone as punishment for a crime   **underdog**: a person or team thought to have little chance of winning

4

Bug Woman and Bird Man

*My childhood dream was to live with wild animals all my life
and to marry a tall, dark man.*

—Fran Hamerstrom

When Fran was 21, she was invited to a party at Dartmouth College. Her date had to cancel, so he asked a friend to take Fran to the party instead. That friend was Frederick Hamerstrom.

Fran and Frederick spent the night happily dancing. They both said they fell in love on that very first date. In the fall of 1928, after 3 dates, they became secretly engaged.

The next year, Frederick **transferred** to Harvard University, near Boston, to be closer to Fran. Frederick **majored** in English, which helped him later in life with his many writing projects. But his grades fell because he was spending so much time

transferred (**trans** furd): moved from one place to another   **majored**: specialized in a particular subject at a college or university

with Fran. Instead of studying on the weekends, he and Fran explored the outdoors and went hunting and fishing together. They both especially loved hunting birds and would often observe and learn from older bird hunters. They realized they wanted their future life together to include hunting and working outdoors with wild animals.

In November 1930, Fran and Frederick announced their engagement. Fran's parents worried that Frederick could not support their daughter. Still, her parents planned a large, fancy June wedding at their home.

In February, 4 months before the wedding, Fran and Frederick took a trip to Florida. While in Florida, they decided to get married there. They knew their families had their hearts set on a beautiful wedding, so they kept the marriage a secret. That June, Fran walked down the staircase of her family home for a formal wedding. No one guessed they were already married.

After the wedding, Fran and Frederick decided that if they wanted to work outdoors with wild animals, they needed to learn more about raising **game** animals. In September 1931, they enrolled at a school called the Game Conservation Institute in New Jersey.

HAMERSTROM FAMILY ARCHIVES

The school did not want to admit Fran because she was a woman. As usual, Fran took matters into her own hands. She drove to New York City, where the school board was meeting. She burst into the meeting and convinced the board

Fran and Frederick's formal family wedding

of directors to admit her to the school as their first female student.

game: an animal hunted for sport or for food

23

When Fran and Frederick arrived at the school, the other male students did not accept her at first. But soon Fran found a way to win them over. The old school buildings were full of rats. So one day, the male students organized a rat hunt. The boys drove the rats toward Fran. She caught the rats barehanded and threw them against the floorboards to kill them. After that, she had no more problems with the male students accepting her.

Unfortunately, Fran and Frederick quickly became disappointed with the school. One of their main duties was raising pheasant chicks for hunting. Visitors came to the school to hunt, and the students acted as guides. One day the visiting hunters insisted that the students hang the pheasants in bags to make it easier for them

HAMERSTROM FAMILY ARCHIVES

Fran and Frederick at the Conservation Institute in Clinton, New Jersey to shoot. Fran and Frederick were shocked. While they liked hunting, they thought it was wrong and unfair to shoot birds in bags. They began searching for another way to pursue their interest in the management of wild birds.

In December 1931, Frederick attended a conference in New York City. He heard a speech by a man named Aldo Leopold. The speech was a turning point in Frederick's life.

Leopold spoke about a new type of American conservation that focused on wildlife management. Scientists who believed in wildlife management worked to protect animals and help them adapt to changing environments.

Leopold believed in public hunting rights for everyone. But he also wanted to establish hunting laws to protect animals from overhunting. He encouraged hunters and conservationists to work together to save wildlife from extinction.

Who Was Aldo Leopold?

Aldo Leopold is widely known as the father of wildlife ecology and the modern environmental movement. He was a professor of wildlife management at the University of Wisconsin–Madison. His book *A Sand County Almanac* is one of the most important conservation books ever written.

Aldo Leopold believed that a community is more than a group of people living closely together. A community also includes the animals, plants, fields, woods, soil, and water that surround it. He called this group of living and nonliving things that support each other an **ecosystem**.

Our environment is healthiest when all parts of an ecosystem work well together. If the water becomes

Aldo Leopold

polluted or the soil blows away, the animals, plants, and people on the land all suffer. People are responsible for protecting all parts of the environment. Leopold called his belief a "land **ethic**."

Leopold's conservation principles were very different from what most people believed at the time. Hunters thought it was their right to kill wildlife for food or fun. They didn't realize that

ecosystem (ee koh sis tuhm): the whole group of living and nonliving things that make up an environment and affect each other   **ethic**: a rule of moral behavior governing an individual or group

uncontrolled hunting could lead to extinction of a species. Aldo Leopold trained scientists to manage wildlife so that the animals would not die out.

Leopold convinced the government to protect **spectacular** wilderness areas from development. Without protection, he was afraid wilderness would disappear. He convinced the US Forest Service to establish the **Gila** National Wilderness in New Mexico. It was the first national wilderness area in the country. Leopold and other conservationists founded "The Wilderness Society" to fight for the conservation of wild lands.

Leopold's ideas about conserving our lands and habitats are still the basis of environmental work today. The Aldo Leopold Foundation near Baraboo, Wisconsin, works with groups all over the United States to teach his ideas.

Frederick finally found the right direction for his career. He started looking for jobs in game management. Eventually he got a job with Dr. Paul Errington at Iowa State College. Dr. Errington was head of the first Cooperative Wildlife Research Unit in the United States. Frederick was admitted to the **graduate program** at Iowa State College. Fran also decided to go back to college to finish her **degree**.

---

spectacular (spek **ta** kyuh lur): striking   **Gila: hee** luh   **graduate program**: a school, usually at a university that offers degrees beyond the bachelor's degree   **degree**: title given to students by a college or university

Fran and Frederick did not have a lot of money. So they packed up their car and camped all the way to Iowa. They picked corn from farmers' fields and roasted it for dinner, along with roadkill that they found on the highway. They barely made it to Iowa before their car broke down. When they finally arrived in Ames, Iowa, they moved into an ugly little house. Frederick earned 90 dollars a month for his job. Fran found a part-time job earning 35 cents a day.

Fran and Frederick made the most of their time in Iowa. Though Fran was busy finishing her undergraduate degree, she still found time to help Frederick with his field study projects. Dr. Errington liked Fran and didn't mind it when she joined them on their field trips.

Fran and Frederick spent many days searching for the nests of owls and hawks. They collected thousands of owl **pellets**, which are formed from bones, fur, and feathers. Owls cannot digest the pellets, so they spit them out. Fran and Frederick took apart the pellets to find out what the owls ate.

pellets: wads of material (like bone and fur) that cannot be digested and has been thrown up by a bird of prey

Dr. Errington taught Fran and Frederick how to write accurate field notes of their observations. The **techniques** that Fran and Frederick learned in Iowa helped them in their own research throughout their lives.

Dr. Paul Errington's students studied owl pellets that looked like the one in this illustration.

Fran and Frederick also spent time pursuing their own individual interests. Frederick had a bird and mammal collection in one room of their house, and Fran kept her insect collection in another room. Iowa friends nicknamed them "Bug Woman and Bird Man."

The couple studied at Iowa State for 3 years. Frederick became Dr. Errington's most trusted and valuable assistant. In 1935, Frederick earned his graduate degree in **zoology**. On her second try at college, Fran finally graduated. Frederick's

technique (tek **neek**): a way of doing something using special knowledge or skill   zoology (zoh **ah** luh jee): a branch of biology concerned with the study of animals and animal life

education allowed him to find a job in **Necedah**, in central Wisconsin, managing wildlife. Soon they would leave Iowa and move north.

Best of all, Fran and Frederick became friends with Aldo Leopold during their time in Iowa. They visited Leopold at his home near Baraboo, Wisconsin, which was lovingly known as "the shack." Fran and Frederick's friendship with Leopold became one of the most important friendships of their lives.

Necedah: nuh **see** duh

5
Welcome to Wisconsin

Not for all the capitals in Europe and the wealth of the Indies would I give up what I have now: love, adventure, and public service in the unmapped wilds of central Wisconsin.

—Fran Hamerstrom

In the fall of 1935, Fran and Frederick loaded their car and trailer with all their possessions and drove to their new home in Wisconsin.

At the time, the farmers in central Wisconsin were living in extreme **poverty**. The United States was in the middle of the **Great Depression**. Jobs were scarce. The land in Necedah was poorly suited for growing crops, and farm families barely made a living. Most families earned about $150 a year. To survive, people raised potatoes, gathered nuts and berries, and hunted wild game for food.

poverty (**pov** ur tee): the condition of being poor   **Great Depression**: a time from October 29, 1929, into the 1930s when businesses did badly and many people became poor

31

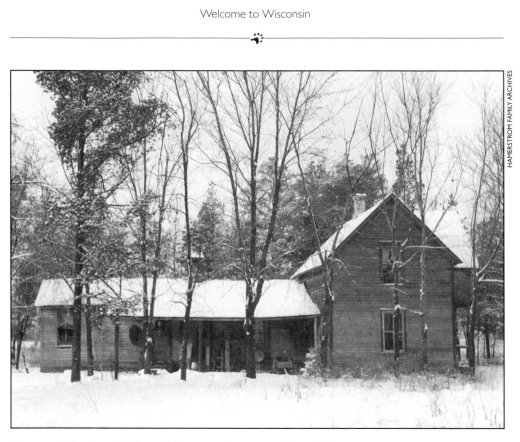

Fran and Frederick's first Wisconsin home in Necedah

People were more worried about their families starving than following game laws. They hunted out of season and took more animals than allowed. Over-hunting had **depleted** the wild game supply. Frederick's job was to find a way to encourage the game population to grow again. That way, game animals would be plentiful for hunting but their survival would not be threatened.

depleted (di **plee** tid): reduced by using up

The Wisconsin Dust Bowl

In the early 1900s, central Wisconsin farmland was a combination of marsh and light sand. The poor soil wasn't very good for growing farm crops. Many farmers could grow only marsh hay to feed small herds of dairy cows. Families sold cranberries, peat moss, and hay to survive.

Land management experts decided to improve the soil by draining off the **excess** water. They dug drainage ditches throughout the marsh. Unfortunately, the drainage ditches made the problem worse. Water in the soil drained out to the

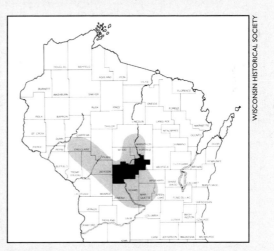

This map shows the parts of Wisconsin most affected by the Dust Bowl.

nearby rivers and streams. The ground dried out so much that fires burned off the top layers of soil and turned it into dust. The sandy soil easily blew away in the strong winds. And the ditches destroyed habitat for birds and plants.

The spring of 1934 was the driest spring in the Midwest for 70 years. In Wisconsin, the biggest dust storm of the **century**

excess (**ek** ses): too much   **century** (**sen** chuh ree): a period of 100 years

33

blew away thousands of acres of soil. Dust and sand buried and destroyed the cropland. The wind blew for 2 days that May, carrying dry soil all the way to the east coast. Stories were told of Wisconsin soil landing on the carpets in the White House in Washington, DC.

Sometimes good things happen as the result of bad events. Farmers learned one important thing from the dust storm of 1934. They learned they needed to plant trees around their fields to slow the winds and help hold the soil in place.

Immediately after the dust storm of 1934, central Wisconsin farmers began to plant rows of jack pines around their fields. The trees would grow quickly and would help keep the soil in place during strong winds. Thanks to the **devastating** dust storm, farmers realized the value of soil conservation.

WHI IMAGE ID 6795

Farmers planted rows of young jack pines around their fields to keep the soil from blowing away.

Frederick worked for President Franklin Roosevelt's Resettlement Administration. The Resettlement Administration helped poor farm families move from

devastating (**dev** uh stay ting): destroying entirely or nearly entirely

unproductive land and resettle elsewhere. The government planned to use the empty land for wildlife refuges and parks. Frederick's job was to find out more about the animals that lived there. Once he knew more about the animals and their needs, he could develop a plan to manage their habitat.

WHI IMAGE ID 98472

This house and barn were abandoned as part of the Resettlement Administration.

Thanks to Frederick's work in Necedah, the area later became a national wildlife area called the Necedah National Wildlife Refuge. It still exists today!

At first, many people in central Wisconsin were suspicious of the idea of creating wildlife refuges. They knew very little about conservation of natural resources. Shooting birds and animals for food or fun was a strong **tradition**.

tradition: belief or custom handed down from one generation to another

35

Passenger pigeons had already been hunted and killed until they became extinct. Most people didn't care about the loss of a species of birds or wild animals. The Hamerstroms soon realized they needed to teach others about the importance of wildlife conservation.

Extinction: The Case of the Passenger Pigeon

WHI IMAGE ID 53469

A passenger pigeon, before the birds became extinct

The passenger pigeon was once the most **abundant** bird in North America. Early settlers **estimated** that between 3 and 5 billion passenger pigeons lived in the United States. People reported seeing flocks of birds so big they blocked out the sun. In the 1800s, the famous **naturalist** John Muir said a migrating flock of passenger pigeons looked like a "mighty river in the sky." One man in Kentucky estimated that a flock he saw was one mile wide and 240 miles long.

No one dreamed it was possible to wipe out such a vast species. But at the time there were no hunting rules, and unlimited

abundant (uh **buhn** duhnt): present in large numbers   **estimated** (**es** tuh may tuhd): gave or formed a general idea of the value, size, or cost of something   **naturalist** (**na** chuh ruh list): person who studies nature and especially plants and animals as they live in nature

36

killing led to its extinction. Martha, the world's last passenger pigeon, died in a zoo in 1914.

How was it possible to kill so many birds?

The passenger pigeons' favorite foods were acorns, nuts, and seeds. As forests were cut down, the pigeons began to eat corn and seeds from farmers' fields. A large flock could ruin a field of crops in minutes. Farmers and landowners shot the birds to keep them from ruining their crops. Pigeon hunters sold them to restaurants and markets for food.

Passenger pigeons were an easy target. The flocks roosted closely together in the woods. One tree could contain 90 nests. Hunters caught them in nets, shot them, and clubbed them. They even set fire to the woods to kill as many birds as possible. Slowly, their numbers began to fall.

In central Wisconsin, the largest nesting ground in history was recorded in 1871. The nesting ground was 850 square miles. Hunters killed more than one million birds and sent them east for food.

In 1947, a memorial to the passenger pigeon was built in Wisconsin's **Wyalusing** State Park on the Mississippi River. Aldo Leopold spoke at the dedication of the monument. He said, "No living man will ever again see the onrushing **phalanx** of **victorious** birds, sweeping a path for spring against the March

Wyalusing: wı uh **loo** sing   **phalanx** (**fay** langks): a large group of people, animals, or things often placed close together   **victorious** (vik **tor** ee uhs): having won a victory

skies, chasing the defeated winter from all the woods and prairies of Wisconsin."

More than anything else, the loss of the passenger pigeon taught scientists the importance of wildlife conservation. Scientists realized that extinction can happen to any species.

This bronze plaque is part of the passenger pigeon monument in Wyalusing State Park.

DEDICATED
TO THE LAST WISCONSIN
PASSENGER PIGEON
SHOT AT BABCOCK, SEPT. 1899
THIS SPECIES BECAME EXTINCT
THROUGH THE AVARICE AND
THOUGHTLESSNESS OF MAN.
ERECTED BY
THE WISCONSIN SOCIETY FOR ORNITHOLOGY

WHI IMAGE ID 34683

Frederick's task was huge. He needed to survey all the animals in the area and then make a plan to help the wildlife population grow. A lack of roads, maps, and equipment made the job very hard. The Hamerstroms and their crew drew the first maps of the area, over 7,000 acres.

President Roosevelt wanted to put as many men to work as he could during the Great Depression. Frederick **supervised** a crew of 500 men. He had never directed more than 2 or 3 workers at one time. Luckily, not all 500 men showed up at

supervised (**soo** pur vɪzd): coordinated and directed the activities of

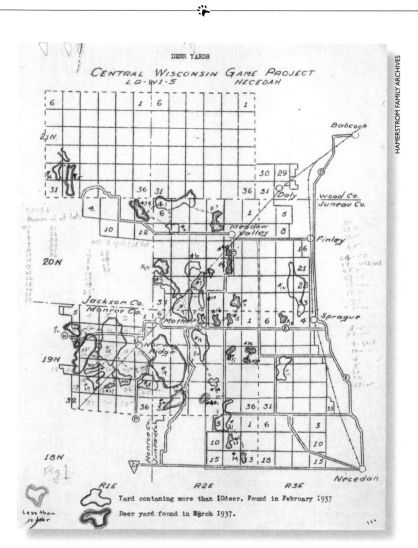

Frederick drew this map of deer yards for the Central Wisconsin Game Project in Necedah.

once, but Frederick still needed to find a way to keep large groups of men busy.

39

Frederick put the men to work counting all the wild animals. Lines of men walked through the woods and marshes. They counted flocks of prairie chickens, game birds, rabbits, deer, and other small mammals. Meanwhile, smaller crews located nesting sites and drew color-coded maps of the wildlife ranges. Frederick asked the government of Wisconsin to set aside parcels of land for the animals' feeding and winter **habitation**.

The Necedah National Wildlife Refuge

The maps that Fran and Frederick created while working in Necedah helped to create the Necedah National Wildlife Refuge in 1939. The refuge sits on the site of the biggest wetland bog in Wisconsin. The area is known as the Great Central Wisconsin Swamp. The bog was formed from a giant lake that drained from glaciers 10,000 years ago.

Today the refuge is a mix of sand dunes, grassland, wetland, and open water. It is the perfect habitat for waterfowl and the largest **stopover** in Wisconsin for migrating sandhill cranes. Other endangered species, such as the Karner blue butterfly and the gray wolf, also live in the Necedah Refuge.

habitation (ha buh **tay** shuhn): the act of living in a place   stopover: stop made during a journey

The refuge is also a home to the endangered whooping crane. In 1980, scientists became very concerned about the whooping cranes. The cranes were close to extinction. Several conservation groups worked together to save them.

In 2001, scientists from the Necedah Refuge, the Wisconsin Department of Natural Resources, the International Crane Foundation, and other conservation organizations worked together to create

Biologists at the Necedah Refuge are working to save endangered whooping cranes like this one.

a flock of wild whooping cranes at the Necedah Refuge. The scientists teach the cranes to breed on their own in the wild and safely migrate to warmer climates in the winter. Thanks to the efforts at Necedah and other refuges throughout the state, there are now about 90 whooping cranes in Wisconsin. If you take a walk through the Necedah Refuge in the spring, you may be lucky enough to see a nesting pair of whooping cranes!

Frederick asked Fran to direct one of the crews, but her work was unpaid. She was able to spend some of her own time on research projects that interested her. She focused on owl life and hawk life on the Necedah marsh. In 1936, she invited neighbors and scientist friends to Thanksgiving dinner. While she cooked dinner, she continued her work of separating owl pellets at another

table. This was Fran's style throughout her life. She combined constant research with **hospitality**.

Fran was satisfied with her life. She was doing valuable work in what then was considered a man's field. Many women of that era were not so lucky. As always, Fran **strove** to prove herself as capable as a man doing the same job. One winter day, Frederick sent her off on her own to finish a game survey. She came to a wide stream and decided the only way to get across was to strip off her clothes, carry them over her head, and swim across the stream. When she reached the other side, she got dressed and ran to warm herself.

hospitality (hahs puh **tal** uh tee): friendly and generous treatment of guests   **strove**: tried very hard

Fran also began writing articles about their research for the local newspapers. She was a talented writer. She thought about her subject carefully before putting the words down on paper, and her work needed very little **editing**. Fran had a gift for explaining scientific material in a way that anyone could understand. It was a practice that she continued throughout her life.

Life for the Hamerstroms in Wisconsin was completely different from the safe, secure world of their childhood, but they loved it. Their old rundown house had no heat and no indoor **plumbing**.

Every day in the winter, Fran and Frederick trudged miles through the snow on snowshoes searching for wildlife. At night, they returned to a freezing house. One of them pumped water from a pump in the yard while the other started a fire in a woodstove to warm up the kitchen. They ate dinner and soon fell into bed in an ice-cold bedroom.

editing: preparation of written material for publication by correcting or modifying it   **plumbing (pluh** ming): system of pipes and fixtures for supplying and carrying off water in a building

One day, when the temperature reached 35 degrees below zero, their pump froze. Neighbors came over to help them. They asked Fran to find some rags to wrap around the pump. She ran upstairs and looked through her suitcases of clothes she had kept from her younger days. She found a gorgeous red velvet ball gown. Fran carried the gown downstairs and handed it to one of the neighbors. The neighbor wrapped the gown around the pump, soaked it in kerosene, and lit it on fire. As she watched her gown burn, Fran realized she would never return to her former life.

Fran described this period of their life as a "wild adventure." She and Frederick were working together outdoors, doing work that they loved. They both clearly realized they were choosing a different lifestyle than what they had as children. Fran said they chose "to move from a narrow, cultured background to a wide, wide world of real people and opportunities."

Eventually, Fran and Frederick decided they could not accomplish all they wanted to do while working for the government. They realized the main purpose of the Resettlement Administration was to put people to work, not to help the animal population. They knew skillful wildlife management would save animals from extinction. And they knew they needed more education in the science of wildlife research.

Their friend Aldo Leopold had just started a new program in game management at the University of Wisconsin-Madison. This would be the best place to learn more about wildlife research.

Fran and Frederick applied, and to their delight they were accepted into the program. Frederick would work on a **PhD** and Fran would become Leopold's first female graduate student. In 1937, they left Necedah for Madison.

PhD: the highest degree given by a graduate program

6

The Wildest of Wild Creatures

The opportunity to see geese is more important than television.

—Aldo Leopold

Aldo Leopold was a tough and demanding teacher. He admitted only 5 students each year into his program. His students had to be independent thinkers with some field experience. Fran and Frederick **thrived** under his teaching. They knew how lucky they were to be able to study under someone like Aldo Leopold.

Leopold took his students on field trips where they carefully observed animals and plants. He insisted that his students keep accurate records of their observations, and he did not tolerate sloppy research or writing. Leopold once said of his own writing, "It takes 7 editings, sometimes 17, before I send it to the press."

thrived (thrīvd): grew or developed very well

46

Leopold became a close friend and **mentor** to Fran and Frederick. They put his teachings into practice for the rest of their lives.

Aldo Leopold, Frederick, and Fran

Fran and Frederick lived in an old farmhouse near Madison. They missed the quiet nights on the marsh in Necedah. They studied for a year and a half in Madison and soaked up Leopold's conservation ideals. But eventually they had to go back to the countryside to conduct research for their graduate project.

mentor: someone who teaches or gives help and advice to a less experienced and often younger person

Leopold assigned them a project studying one of his favorite birds: the endangered prairie chicken. Like passenger pigeons, prairie chickens were once abundant. They were regularly hunted for food. But they began to decline rapidly around 1850.

Two things caused their decline: too much hunting, and the loss of their habitat. Prairie chickens need to live on grasslands for food and nesting grounds. As cities grew and suburbs took over more rural land, the grasslands began to disappear. Prairie chickens lost their nesting grounds and food sources. Now they were close to disappearing forever in Wisconsin.

A prairie chicken on the Buena Vista Grasslands

48

On a bitterly cold Christmas Eve in 1938, Fran and Frederick went to a Christmas party in Madison. After the party, they drove north to a farmhouse in Hancock, Wisconsin, that Leopold had found for them to live in. Fran was still dressed up in **nylons** and high heels. Frederick was in pain from a tooth that had just been pulled.

When they finally reached the farmhouse, they had to break the lock to get into the ice-cold house. They tried to get a fire going in the woodstove, but the chimney was plugged. So they crawled into a cold, damp bed and hoped things would be better in the morning.

Fran and Frederick were back in central Wisconsin doing what they most loved. This time their task was to locate, trap, mark, and count prairie chickens. They needed to learn more about the prairie chickens' habitat. This began their lifelong **crusade** to save the prairie chicken from extinction.

nylons (nɪ lahnz): stockings   **crusade**: campaign to get things changed for the better

What Is a Prairie Chicken?

Fran and Frederick studied the greater prairie chicken. Though it looks like a chicken, it is really a member of the **grouse** family. Grouse are game birds often prized by hunters. Four species of grouse live in Wisconsin: the ruffed grouse, the sharp-tailed grouse, the spruce grouse, and the greater prairie chicken. The prairie chicken and the sharp-tailed grouse live mainly on grasslands, and the ruffed grouse and spruce grouse live in the woods.

For most of the year, the prairie chicken is a quiet bird with brown and white stripes. But in the spring, the male prairie chickens put on a dramatic, colorful show to attract the females. In the world of prairie chickens, spring is known as "**booming season**."

The scientific name for the prairie chicken is *Tympanuchus cupido pinnatus*. The name means "the drummer of love." The male chicken's booming call sounds like a drum, and the males' feet also beat out a drumming

Two male prairie chickens establish their territory.

grouse (grous): a brownish bird, mostly in wooded areas, that feeds especially on the ground and is sometimes hunted for food or sport   **booming season**: the time of year, usually late March through April, when male prairie chickens perform their displays in hopes of attracting females   **Tympanuchus cupido pinnatus**: tim **pan** uh kuhs **kyu** puh doh   pi **na** tuhs sound as they stomp and dance around the female hens. As they make their booming calls, the bright orange air sacs on the sides of their necks inflate with air. Their 3-inch neck feathers, called pinnae, stand straight up. The males charge each other, jump high into the air, and fight to establish their **territory**.

One **subspecies** of the prairie chicken, the heath hen, is now extinct. It was plentiful on the East Coast when the **Pilgrims** arrived in the United States. The early settlers hunted it for food. Some people believe the Pilgrims ate heath hen, not turkey, at the first Thanksgiving dinner!

Fran and Frederick had a lot to learn about prairie chickens. Their first problem was to find the chickens. Small flocks of prairie chickens were scattered throughout the surrounding marsh. No one knew for sure where they were. Finally, a neighbor told them he had seen some flocks in the cornfields of the Leola marsh, 7 miles away.

Fran and Frederick also needed to figure out the best way to trap the chickens. They set out live traps so they could catch the birds, slip bands around their legs, and then release them. On many cold winter days, they drove to the marsh,

territory: area that is occupied and defended by an animal or group of animals   **subspecies** (**suhb** spee seez): a group of related plants or animals that is smaller than a species   **Pilgrims**: English colonists who founded the first permanent settlement in New England in 1620

strapped on snowshoes, and split up to check the traps. Twice a day they walked the trap lines. They didn't want the prairie chickens to be left in the traps any longer than necessary.

Frederick removes a prairie chicken from a trap to band it.

Fran often said the prairie chicken was the wildest animal of all. They did not like to be trapped. Fran and Frederick experimented with different kinds of traps. They made their first traps out of wire mesh. They were a disaster. The prairie chickens thrashed around in the traps. Sometimes they hurt their wings or scraped and tore their skin.

So Fran and Frederick designed a new trap made out of netting that would not hurt the birds. Fran hauled out her *Encyclopedia of **Embroidery*** and found directions to make netting out of string. Soon she had enough netting to cover 2 traps. But she made a big mistake when she decided to dye the netting. She chose an olive green color and used salt to set the dye. The next day, upon checking the traps, Fran discovered that the salt had attracted deer, squirrels, and rabbits. The animals had eaten big holes in the netting!

Fran and Frederick needed to band the birds so they could keep track of them. The bands were tiny metal strips with numbers that Fran and Frederick put on the birds' legs. The bands had numbers that identified each bird.

Fran and Frederick had problems capturing the birds safely so they could be banded. At first, they tried putting the birds into socks to hold them for a short while. But the birds died if handled too roughly. Wearing gloves caused them to pull

embroidery (im **broi** dur ee): needlework done to decorate cloth

out feathers from the prairie chickens' legs. They learned to handle the chickens with bare hands. It was more important for the chickens to keep their feathers on their legs for warmth than for Fran and Frederick to have warm hands.

Fran and Frederick had to observe the prairie chickens without scaring them away. So they set up a blind, or a small compartment they could hide in. Their first blind was a folding card table covered with a blanket. They arranged peepholes in the blanket so they could see the birds. They tied the blankets down, but the fabric still flapped in the wind and scared the birds away. Eventually, they built small wooden blinds and covered them with canvas.

Fran and Frederick used blinds like this one to observe the prairie chickens on the Buena Vista Grasslands.

One day Aldo Leopold came for a visit. He told them they needed a way to tell the older birds from the young birds. A few days later, Fran remembered the advice an old gamekeeper had given her many years earlier. He had told her, "The best way to kill game birds is to bite them in the head right behind their ears."

So Fran picked up a live bird and bit into its skull behind the ears. To her surprise, the bird dropped dead. After killing a few birds this way, she realized that some skulls were hard and some were soft. Old birds had hard skulls and young birds had soft skulls. She was eager to tell Aldo Leopold that she had discovered a way to age birds!

For a while, Fran and Frederick offered to pluck the feathers of other hunters' prairie chickens so they could add the information on each chicken to their research. Fran usually ended the plucking by biting each dead chicken in the head to determine its age. She startled quite a few hunters with her research technique. Years later, on a journey down the Amazon River in South America, she used the same technique to kill birds.

The Hamerstroms were very poor during these years. They scavenged wood and straightened out old bent nails to build their traps. Just as their neighbors did, they hunted their own food and cut wood to heat their house.

Still, it was a happy time. Aldo Leopold often came and visited them. They liked to hunt prairie chickens and other grouse and cook them over an open fire outdoors. Fran and Frederick were writing their **theses**. Fran's graduate research project was about chickadees and Frederick's was about prairie chickens. They gathered data and spent hours writing their research reports. In 1940, Fran became the first and only woman to earn a graduate degree in wildlife management under Aldo Leopold. Frederick earned his PhD shortly afterward.

theses (thee seez): essays presenting results of original research

7
Family Life and the War Years

We do not own our children, our children own themselves.

—Fran and Frederick Hamerstrom

Fran and Frederick wanted to have a family. In 1940, their first child, Alan, was born. Fran and Frederick planted 1,000 pine trees to celebrate his birth. Fran did not take life easier while she was pregnant. In fact, she went hunting the day Alan was born.

Their life after Alan's birth didn't change much. Fran and Frederick continued their fieldwork and took Alan along. Sometimes when they were working in the field, they left the baby in a basket on top of their car. Two years later, when their daughter Elva was born, they planted another 1,000 trees in her honor.

In 1941, after Fran and Frederick completed their graduate degrees, Frederick began to look for a new job. The University of Michigan offered Frederick a job as a **curator** of a nature reserve. Though he was sad to leave their prairie chicken research, he needed the money for his growing family. He accepted the job, and the family moved to Pinckney, Michigan, near Ann Arbor.

Elva, Fran, Frederick, and Alan in Michigan

curator (**kyoor** ay tur): a person in charge of a museum or zoo

Luckily, Frederick was allowed to return to Wisconsin each spring for the annual prairie chicken booming season. Two weeks after Elva's birth in 1943, Fran and Frederick took her to Wisconsin for the annual prairie chicken count.

Fran and Frederick's life in Michigan was interrupted by World War II. Much to Fran's dismay, Frederick decided to enlist in the army in 1943. Fran didn't want to be left behind. So she packed up the children and followed him.

Frederick worked in El Paso, Texas, as an equipment manager for the bomber crews. He trained the crewmen in safety and efficiency. He performed his duties with his typical attention to detail. In 1945, he was discharged, and the family returned to Michigan.

When World War II ended, Fran and Frederick heard that many German scientists were suffering. The German people had little food or clothing. Many scientists had lost their homes. Both Fran and Frederick became involved in a relief effort they called "The Action." They asked American scientists to help them send care packages to scientists in Germany and across Europe.

Alan and Elva helped their parents gather food and clothing and send it overseas. The German families sent tracings of their feet so the Americans could find the right size shoes to fit. Fran and Frederick used their own savings to buy some of the goods. The Action took over their lives from 1945 until 1948. In all, they helped send more than 3,000 packages to scientists all over Europe.

After The Action ended, the Hamerstroms kept in touch with many German scientists, who became lifelong friends. They even arranged to have their children visit each other's families. Both Elva and Alan lived with German families for a year while they were growing up.

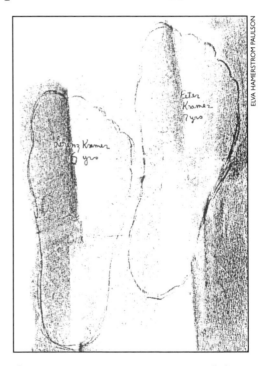

German scientists sent tracings of their families' feet to the Hamerstroms so they could estimate the correct shoe sizes.

The Hamerstroms' parenting style was different from that of many parents of the time. Fran's favorite parenting quote was, "Remember, you don't own your children." Rather than give up their own passions and activities, Fran and Frederick included their children in most of their activities. For example, Alan and Elva learned to help with hunting and trapping chores.

Fran and Frederick's work was hard and constant. Their research continued 7 days a week. There was little time for family leisure. On rare occasions, they all went fishing or roller-skating together.

Fran and Frederick found time to share their own love of the natural world with their children. Fran and the children took nighttime walks when the moon was full.

Because of her own childhood, Fran encouraged her children to have wild pets. Elva's pets included a great horned owl named Minerva, a ferret named Domino, a black rabbit, a jumping mouse, a bat, and numerous snails. On top of this, Fran often had a raptor in the barn

and an owl in the house. Cages of mice were stacked around the house, ready to feed the raptors and bait the traps.

Fran and Frederick were determined to raise their children to be independent. In 1954, Fran and Frederick were invited to visit Finland for a couple of months. They told 11-year-old Elva that she would stay with her grandmother in Boston while they were gone.

Elva had other ideas. She was caring for a bird known as a **Swainson's** hawk. Elva knew she could not take the hawk to her grandmother's house. Her friend Nancy had a chicken coop with an attic. She and Nancy swept the attic and made a bedroom. They

Elva and her pet owl Minerva

Swainson's: swayn suhnz

62

convinced Nancy's mother to let them sleep there at night. Elva could go home during the day to care for her hawk. When she told Fran and Frederick her plans, they agreed.

Fran and Frederick often had guests for dinner. Fran's cooking was **legendary**. Visitors were never sure what she might serve. She was known for cooking very rare meat that oozed blood. She even had a recipe for road-killed snake. She was famous for her pies, preferably made with a crust of bear **lard** and flour.

Guests loved to visit. They were included in whatever activity was going on at the time. They helped feed a hawk or eagle, cooked, did the dishes, or played music. The house was full of laughter and conversation.

In the winter, there were often long periods of quiet family time without visitors. Bookshelves lined the walls of the study from floor to ceiling. Piles of magazines were stacked on the floor. When the family ate dinner without visitors, they usually each read at the table.

legendary (**le** juhn der ee): very famous   **lard**: soft white fat sometimes used for cooking

Though their children were thriving, Fran and Frederick were never very happy during their time in Michigan. Their hearts were still back in central Wisconsin, where they longed to continue working with the prairie chickens. A startling phone call was about to change their lives.

8

Boomers in the Spring

When one tugs at a single thing in nature, he finds it attached to the rest of the world.

—John Muir

In the spring of 1948, Fran and Frederick received a heartbreaking phone call. Their dear friend Aldo Leopold had died of a heart attack while fighting a grass fire. His death helped Fran and Frederick decide to return to Wisconsin. Frederick left his job at the University of Michigan. He and Fran began to look for new jobs.

In the fall of 1949, they were offered jobs with the Wisconsin Conservation Department. Today we call this the Department of Natural Resources, or DNR. Fran and Frederick were hired to manage Wisconsin's grouse program. They were back in the prairie chicken business.

DALE PAULSON

A prairie chicken in its nesting grounds

The prairie chicken had already disappeared in many other states. Some people thought it was too late to save them in Wisconsin. But the Hamerstroms disagreed. They relied on advice they once received from Aldo Leopold. The prairie chicken needed large areas of grassland for survival. Because of this, the birds would respond to land management techniques more than any other species.

The Hamerstrom family's new home was an abandoned farmhouse near Plainfield, Wisconsin, that had been built before the Civil War. They were thrilled. The house was unpainted, and Fran wanted to keep it that way. This was their home for the rest of their lives.

HAMERSTROM FAMILY ARCHIVES

Fran and Frederick's home in Plainfield

Fran and Frederick never installed indoor plumbing. Water for dishes, baths, and drinking came from a pump in an unheated room. When the children were young, Fran and Frederick heated water once a week for their baths. Later, they dug an outdoor pond used for bathing and swimming during warm weather. Guests were warned not to sneak up on Fran, who liked to skinny-dip in the pond.

Three woodstoves heated the house. The lack of plumbing and furnace never bothered the Hamerstroms. Outside activities were much more important to them than a fancy house.

Fran and Frederick had to start all over learning about the prairie chickens. First they trapped and banded the birds. This would help them track each individual bird and learn their habits.

An illustration of the pump room attached to the Hamerstroms' home

Each bird they trapped received at least 2 bands and sometimes more. The first band was an official federal bird band, made of aluminum, that identified each bird with a **unique** number. But these numbers were small and difficult to read with **binoculars**. So the Hamerstroms also used

unique (yoo **neek**): being the only one of its kind for seeing at a distance   binocular (buh **nah** kyuh lur): hand-held instrument used

68

different-colored plastic bands on one or both legs. The different-colored bands identified the trapping grounds where the birds were banded. Large numbers on the plastic bands helped Fran and Frederick easily identify every individual bird, even from far away.

Binoculars

Spring was the busiest time of year for Fran and Frederick. This was the season when prairie chickens came to the booming grounds to find a mate. At one time, there were more than 80 booming grounds all over central Wisconsin. Fran and Frederick monitored about 10 booming grounds close to

Fran bands a prairie chicken.

their home. The booming grounds were meadows of short-mowed grass. Here the males could easily display their **plumage** and attract female hens to them. After mating season was over, the chickens nested in areas with longer grass at the edges of the fields.

Fran and Frederick needed the help of many observers to sit in blinds and record information about the chickens. The data they gathered helped them learn about the prairie chickens' life cycle.

The Hamerstroms' big farmhouse held enough beds for 23 guests. Over the years, Fran and Frederick welcomed more than 7,000 volunteers to their home during the annual booming season. Frederick and Fran nicknamed their volunteer helpers the "boomers."

The schedule during booming season was exhausting. A new group of boomers arrived each evening at 7:30 p.m. At 7:45, Frederick explained the next day's duties. He told the boomers what to look for and how to record it. Fran and Frederick assigned their best boomers to the busiest blinds.

plumage (**ploo** mij): the feathers of a bird

70

Boomers went straight to bed after the briefing and woke up the next morning at 3 a.m. Fran made scrambled eggs, bacon, toast, and coffee every morning. Right after breakfast, the boomers left for the blinds. They were dropped off at the edge of the field and given directions to find the blind in the early morning dark. They needed to get settled before sunup, when the prairie chickens arrived, because any noise from the blinds would scare away the birds.

The boomers usually heard their first birds as dawn broke. They heard the cackling sounds and rustling around the blind before they saw the birds. A few males appeared first. They began booming and drumming their feet. Soon after, the hens appeared. The males became more spirited. They inflated their orange sacs, flew at each other, and jumped straight up in the air.

On a good day, about 20 prairie chickens visited the booming grounds. The action was intense for about an hour or 2, and then the birds began to drift away.

Volunteers were busy recording data during this time. They brought their own binoculars to help them read the band numbers on the chickens. The band numbers

A male prairie chicken with its orange neck sacs inflated and its pinnae raised

helped them keep track of the movement of the individual chickens. The volunteers also counted the birds so they would know if the population was growing or declining. They counted the number of successful matings.

Volunteers drew maps that showed the birds' territories on the booming grounds. **Dominant** males often held positions in the middle of the booming ground. Less-dominant males stayed near the edges.

dominant (**dom** uh nuhnt): controlling or being more powerful or important than all others

The booming activity usually died down around 7 a.m. Volunteers returned to the house, where Fran made a second meal of toasted cheese sandwiches and coffee. Frederick looked over each volunteer's notes and entered all the data into a master record book. After that, the boomers' job was done and they were free to leave.

Fran and Frederick tried to grab a short nap before they began preparing for the next batch of volunteers. This frantic pace continued for at least 6 weeks

Fran and Frederick's volunteers used observation sheets like this one to record what they saw.

every year, from early April to mid-May. Fran and Frederick stayed so busy that they usually each lost 10 pounds during booming season.

For almost 30 years, the Hamerstroms collected data during booming season. They became experts on prairie chickens. They knew the individual chickens, where they nested, where their territories were, what booming grounds they usually went to, and how long they lived. All this data helped them better understand the prairie chickens.

Fran and Frederick's work proved that the prairie chickens could not survive more loss of habitat. The grasslands the prairie chickens depended on were disappearing. The Hamerstroms knew the next step was to convince other people that grasslands needed to be preserved so the prairie chickens would still have a place to live.

9
The Battle for the Chickens

Conservation is a state of harmony between man and the land.

—Aldo Leopold

Land use was a hot topic in Wisconsin in the late 1940s and early 1950s. Large agricultural companies brought huge **irrigation** systems into the marshes. Farmers thought they could finally make a decent living on the sands of central Wisconsin. But conservationists like Fran and Frederick pushed hard to save some land for wildlife.

The Hamerstroms knew the prairie chickens would become extinct if the birds lost their homes. Hens needed a safe place to nest and lay their eggs. So Fran and Frederick proposed a plan that they believed would work well with the agricultural needs of the area. Frederick called his plan a "scatter land management plan."

irrigation (ir uh **gay** shuhn): supplying with water

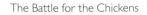

They focused on the Buena Vista marsh in central Wisconsin. The marsh was the perfect place for prairie chickens. It had acres of bluegrass, which was the prairie chicken's favorite food and nesting material.

This is what the Buena Vista Grasslands looks like today.

Frederick wanted to buy 40-acre parcels of land scattered throughout the marsh. The Wisconsin Conservation Department would then manage the parcels so the prairie chickens would always have nesting grounds.

The prairie chicken land would be surrounded by private farmland. Because the prairie chicken land could be scattered in a random pattern, the Hamerstroms thought farmers and prairie chickens could live together peacefully. Frederick wanted to work with the farmers. He believed, like Aldo Leopold, that environmentalists and farmers should be partners in conservation.

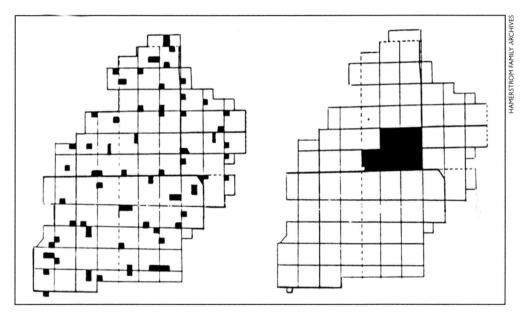

Frederick drew this map to show the difference between his scatter land management plan (on the left) and the traditional method of keeping bird habitat all in one place (on the right).

Fran and Frederick didn't have the money to buy the land themselves. They turned to friends and private conservation groups for help. Friends bought the first pieces of land that were set aside for the prairie chickens.

More contributions came from conservation organizations. The Wisconsin Conservation League, the Wisconsin Society for **Ornithology**, and the Dane County Conservation League bought more than 4,000 acres for prairie chicken lands. In 1961, a group of friends from Milwaukee formed the Society of Tympanuchus Cupido Pinnatus. The society bought more than 7,000 scattered acres of prairie chicken habitat in the Buena Vista marsh. Many years later, in 1989, the society sold its land back to the DNR.

Frederick's dream came true. For the first time in Wisconsin history, the state managed public land in the middle of private farmland. Today, the Wisconsin DNR still manages the land for the prairie chickens.

ornithology (or nuh **thah** luh jee): a branch of science that deals with the study of birds

In the beginning, Frederick's plan was widely misunderstood. In the 1950s, people were still suspicious about the idea of preserving habitat to save wildlife.

An argument broke out between the conservationists and a group of farmers in central Wisconsin. The farmers were angry because they were afraid the state could force them to sell their land for prairie chicken habitat. Local landowners and farmers had several meetings to discuss Frederick's plan. Frederick spoke up at the meetings to try to **reassure** the landowners that the state was not going to take their land.

It was a difficult time for the Hamerstroms. Neighbors looked at them with doubt and mistrust. They were nicknamed "the chicken people."

Even though Fran and Frederick had lived in Wisconsin for 20 years, their New England accents made them sound like outsiders. Rumors **circulated** about their strange lifestyle. People didn't understand why the Hamerstroms lived in an old house with no plumbing. Fran was once again criticized

---

reassure (ree uh **shur**): to make someone feel less afraid, upset, or doubtful **circulated** (**sur** kyuh lay tid): passed from place to place or from person to person

because she was a woman doing a man's work. She dressed strangely and often went barefoot. She had even been spotted climbing trees! It got so bad that when their son Alan put a pirate flag on top of the house, neighbors accused them of flying a **foreign** flag and whispered that they were spies.

During those years, Fran and Frederick were often called on to educate the public about the needs of the prairie chickens. They did everything they could to spread their message of habitat conservation. They wrote articles for newspapers and even went on television to talk about the prairie chickens.

Slowly, their hard work began to pay off. Neighbors who admired the Hamerstroms spoke up on their behalf. People began to understand that they were responsible for caring for the wildlife and land around them.

Gradually, the public became more comfortable with Frederick's land management plan. Farmers and environmentalists began to see they could both have what they wanted. They could all survive and thrive together.

foreign (for uhn): belonging to another place or country

Slowly, conservationists bought more land in the marsh for prairie chicken management. Eventually, they preserved about 12,000 acres in the Buena Vista marsh for prairie chicken habitat.

A sign at the Buena Vista Grasslands

The Buena Vista Grasslands

In the 1800s, the Buena Vista Grasslands in central Wisconsin was a wetland made up of **tamarack** swamps and open marsh. Settlers gradually cut down the trees and dug drainage ditches throughout the marsh. Bluegrass, a favorite food for prairie chickens, began to grow until it covered half the marsh. The other half of the marsh was a mix of cropland, pasture, and woodlands.

The Hamerstroms' land management plan created a permanent habitat at the Buena Vista Grasslands for prairie chickens. Their plan is still used today. In fact, the scatter land management plan is used throughout the United States as a model for other wildlife conservation programs.

The Buena Vista Grasslands provides the perfect habitat for prairie chickens. The chickens love to eat the bluegrass seeds and hide their nests in the tall grass. The corn crops raised by the farmers on the marsh also provide food and shelter in the winter. The open croplands provide booming grounds in the spring.

The Buena Vista Grasslands area is managed by the Wisconsin Department of Natural Resources. Each spring volunteers still come to the marsh to count chickens in the annual prairie chicken count.

tamarack (**tam** uh rak): a type of tree that is related to the pines and that drops its needles in the winter

10

Raptor Love

Two harriers are sky-dancing over the marsh.

—Fran Hamerstrom

Throughout her life, Fran worked with Frederick to save the prairie chickens. But she always made time to pursue her lifelong passion for raptors. Raptors are birds of prey that kill other animals for food. Raptors such as hawks, owls, and eagles all fascinated her.

Fran's love of raptors began when she was a young girl and held her pet kestrel in her hand. Later, she joined the North American Falconers Association. Falconers train birds of prey to hunt other animals. Fran devoted herself to learning how to raise raptors and train them successfully. Both Fran and Frederick believed in learning by closely observing the animals they studied.

Fran served as a chairperson for the North American Falconers Association for 7 years. She and Frederick helped write some of the first federal laws that legalized the sport of falconry.

Fran was one of the first women in the United States to get a permit to band eagles. One day a group of 5 teenage boys drove up to Fran's house in Plainfield. The boys had driven from Rockford, Illinois. They needed a person with a Wisconsin banding permit to help them trap eagles. They decided to ask Fran for help.

Fran flies her eagle.

Fran liked the spirit of the young boys and thought it would be fun to help them. She nicknamed them the Rockford Bunch.

Fran discovered that the boys knew a lot about raptors. She became a regular partner in their birding adventures. If the boys called and said they needed her help, she jumped into her red **Volkswagen** van to help them catch and band raptors. She became a close friend and mentor to the boys. In later years, members of the Rockford Bunch helped the Hamerstroms with their research projects.

Much of Fran's knowledge of birds came from living closely with them and observing their habits. Fran had a natural sense of how to care for birds. Neighbors and other birders often called her when they found hurt or ill raptors. Fran learned to nurse them back to health. If the birds were very young, she imitated the actions of a mother bird. She put the baby birds under her shirt to keep them warm. She chewed scraps of meat to soften them and then popped the meat into the baby bird's mouth.

The Hamerstrom barn was the perfect home for injured raptors. Fran took care of the birds inside the barn and trained them to hunt. Later, as the birds became stronger, she took them outside to fly. The birds needed to practice flying so they could return to the wild and live on their own.

Volkswagen: voks wa guhn

Raptor Rehabilitation

Raptor **rehabilitators** care for sick and injured birds of prey. The goal of rehabilitation is to return the bird to the wild as soon as it can survive on its own. A raptor rehabilitator usually works with a wildlife veterinarian to heal the bird. The rehabilitator then retrains the bird to fly and hunt. If the training is successful, the rehabilitator takes the raptor to an appropriate habitat and releases it.

In the United States, raptor rehabilitators must be licensed. A rehabilitator has to have many different skills. They must know the bird's natural habitat and diet, and what it needs to survive in the wild. They need to know how to exercise the bird so it will regain muscle strength. Handling the bird correctly is important. Raptors' wings can easily be broken from improper handling. Rehabilitators are often trained falconers who know how to teach a raptor to fly and hunt.

Raptors need plenty of space. They need protection from outside predators and bad weather. And they need specialized perches for their feet. Wire is never used for a perch because it can cut the raptor's feet.

Raptors eat a lot of food. They prefer live mice, rats, fish, or chicken. Rehabilitators can't be **squeamish** about watching a bird gulp down a live animal.

rehabilitator (ree uh **bil** uh tay tur): a person who helps to bring someone or something back to a normal, healthy condition after an illness or injury   **squeamish** (**skwee** mish): hesitant because of shock or disgust

When the bird is ready for release, the rehabilitator works with wildlife experts to prepare the raptor for its return to the wild. It's both a happy time and a sad time when the rehabilitator releases the bird and watches it fly away, free again.

For several years, Fran attempted to **breed** a young golden eagle, Chrys, to bear baby eagles. Fran was very patient, but she never succeeded in breeding Chrys. Eventually, she gave Chrys to Cornell University. A few years later a biologist at Cornell used Fran's research to successfully breed Chrys. The baby eaglet thrived.

Nancy, a golden eagle, was another of Fran's favorites. Fran began caring for Nancy when a friend asked for help. Nancy was covered in ticks and very sick. It took Fran several years to train Nancy to hunt well enough to release her into the wild. Finally, when Fran knew she was ready, she drove to Wyoming to release her in the best possible place for Nancy's survival.

breed: produce or increase animals or plants by sexual reproduction

Through the years, Fran also kept owls. The family's screened front porch made a perfect owl cage. Fran's pet great horned owl, **Ambrose**, sometimes sat at the dinner table with the Hamerstroms and their guests.

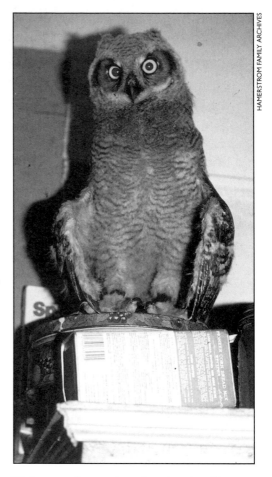

HAMERSTROM FAMILY ARCHIVES

Frederick encouraged Fran to pursue her own research projects. Over the years, she conducted long-term studies of birds such as harriers, kestrels, and ospreys. In 1957, Fran began a 27-year project involving harriers, or marsh hawks. She wanted

This great horned owl makes itself comfortable in Fran and Frederick's kitchen.

to answer the question, "Do harriers mate for life?" She discovered that harriers do not mate for life but often have 2 or even 3 different partners.

Ambrose: am brohz

Fran used her owl, Ambrose, as bait in her research, but she was careful to protect Ambrose from getting hurt. First she tied Ambrose to a perch beneath a fine-mesh net. When a harrier flew over and spotted the owl, it swooped down, flew into the net, and was caught. As soon as the harrier was caught, an observer ran out to capture the bird before it untangled itself.

One problem Fran studied during her harrier research was the effect of DDT on the bird populations. DDT is a chemical that was sprayed over fields to kill mosquitoes and elm bark beetles. Fran's research clearly showed that birds died in large numbers wherever DDT was used. Fran and Frederick joined other scientists in an effort to ban the use of DDT in Wisconsin. In 1969, Wisconsin became the first state to ban DDT.

WHI IMAGE ID 60301

Two workers spray DDT into tall grass. Thanks to Fran and Frederick's work, the government later banned this harmful chemical.

Three years later, the United States completely banned all agricultural use of DDT.

In 1968, Fran realized that in 20 years, she had seen only 3 kestrel nests in the area. She worried that the lack of nesting sites in central Wisconsin limited the growth of the kestrel population. So she began a 25-year project to study kestrels. She and her volunteers put up 50 kestrel nest boxes. They began keeping records of the kestrel population. Kestrels soon adopted many of her nest boxes. Fran's Central Wisconsin Kestrel Research still continues today. It is the longest-running kestrel project in the United States.

How did Fran have the time to do the volume of research needed for these long-term projects? For more than 25 years, more than 100 volunteers from all over the world worked with Fran on her research projects. She nicknamed her helpers the "gabboons."

Gabboons usually spent summers with the Hamerstroms. Their duties included trapping and banding kestrels, harriers, and short-eared owls. They put up kestrel boxes. They helped with record-keeping tasks such as counting the vole population. They located and counted raptors such as marsh hawks, red-tailed hawks, kestrels, sharp-shinned hawks, and Cooper's hawks.

Gabboons didn't just do scientific work. They worked on whatever was needed around the house. They helped with yard work and chores, did simple carpentry, hauled wood, and built traps. They learned practical skills as well as scientific ones.

Sometimes they helped pick up roadkill to feed to Fran's eagles and owls. Fran kept an extra freezer for storing the meat. Once a neighbor called Fran to tell her a cow had died and she could have it for her birds of prey. She and a couple of gabboons jumped in her red van and took off to pick up the cow. They hooked it up to the back of the van and dragged it home.

At lunch, Fran and Frederick held "roundtables" at which they discussed the scientific methods the gabboons were using in the field. They also taught the gabboons a few

M. ROSS LIEN

Gabboon Gary Anweiler naps with an owl over his head.

basic rules of manners. "Never tip back in a chair" was one of Fran's important rules.

Often, the gabboons were attending graduate school and conducting research. They were writing their graduate theses while living with the Hamerstroms. Fran and Frederick edited the students' paperwork. They were demanding teachers and insisted on accuracy. They taught their gabboons excellent writing skills and solid scientific research, just as their teacher Aldo Leopold had taught them.

Christine Thomas, dean of the College of Natural Resources at the University of Wisconsin–Stevens Point, once said this about Fran and Frederick's mentorship: "Those who came to Fran and Frederick were schooled in many things. They learned the lessons of wildlife. They learned simple living. They learned what it means to 'walk the walk' with the courage of their **convictions**. If they needed it, they were schooled in table manners."

Many gabboons went on to have notable careers in science. Fran and Frederick kept in close touch with their gabboons as they pursued their careers. The Hamerstroms' influence spread throughout the world.

conviction (kuhn **vik** shuhn): a strong belief or opinion

11

Those Who Capture the Doves

The Hamerstroms were always looking for answers. It occupied every hour of the day, every day of the week, every week of the month. It was a never-ending quest which took place on the marsh, in the laboratory, and even on the dance floor.

—Dan Trainer

In 1971 Fran and Frederick received an important award. They were given the Distinguished Service Award for Wildlife Conservation from a famous organization known as the National Wildlife Federation.

One year later, the Hamerstroms retired from the DNR. They now had free time to travel. They spent winters in Texas at the Welder Wildlife Refuge, where they banded Harris hawks and wrote articles and books. Sometimes they traveled farther south to Mexico to study ospreys. In Mexico, their camp was very close to the **Seri** Indian Reservation, and

Seri: se ree

they made friends with many of the native residents. The Seri community nicknamed them "those who capture the doves." They called Fran "the old woman who looks for birds."

All their lives, Fran and Frederick had been happy working together. They supported each other's strengths and weaknesses. They ignored traditional roles for men and women. Frederick planned and supervised the fieldwork and research, wrote reports, and kept in touch with fellow scientists throughout the world. He insisted on getting all research accurate

HAMERSTROM FAMILY ARCHIVES

Frederick in his 70s

and perfect. A task took him 4 times as long as it took Fran. Friends described him as the steady, solid half of the couple.

Everyone who knew Frederick respected him for his honesty and warmth.

As a woman scientist, Fran had a tougher path. Her strength was her ability to describe nature in a way that people understood. She wrote popular books about her adventures with eagles, owls, and harriers. She loved telling stories and didn't always stick to the facts, as Frederick did. Frederick was calm and thoughtful, but Fran was lively and energetic. She never hesitated to jump in her Volkswagen van to rescue a bird or a friend in need.

Fran and Frederick continued to invite friends and fellow scientists to their home. They loved when people stopped by for a chat so they could talk about their latest research or adventure. Their dinner table was often filled with lively conversation.

The Hamerstroms' lifestyle served as a model for simple living. Like Aldo Leopold, they spent their lives close to the land, observing the birds and animals around them.

"Their main requirement was to be true in all you do," said their close friend **Deann De La Rhonde**. "Frederick was the **rudder**, Fran the wind, while on sailed the ship."

Sadly, in March 1990, Frederick died of cancer. In his last weeks, he and Fran moved to a small cabin on a river in Oregon near their daughter, Elva. The Hamerstroms' long partnership of 59 years had ended.

Fran missed her husband. But true to her spirit, she tried to live the rest of her life as well as she could without him. Frederick had never liked warm weather, but Fran loved it. So she traveled to **Zaire** and hunted with the **Pygmies**. Because she was in her 80s, she prepared for the trip by getting herself as fit as possible. She trained in Texas, where she ran and climbed trees to get in shape. She studied **Swahili** and French so she could speak to the natives. In Africa, she pitched her pup tent and camped next to the Pygmy homes. She lost 27 pounds while hunting with them.

Deann De La Rhonde: dee an de luh **rohnd**   **rudder**: a movable flat piece attached at the rear of a ship or aircraft for steering   **Zaire** (zah **ir**): a Central African state, now known as the Democratic Republic of the Congo   **Pygmies** (**pig** meez): members of a group of very small people who live in Africa   **Swahili** (swah **hee** lee): a language widely used in East Africa and the Congo region

Fran also traveled to **Dubai** to visit a former gabboon who had become the falconer to a **sheik**. At the age of 86, she took her first trip to the jungles of **Peru**, where she traveled down the Amazon River in a dugout canoe. She broke her hip in Peru, but she went back the following year.

In her last years, Fran continued to journey south in the winter and come home to Plainfield in the summer. She kept busy with writing projects, gardening, and enjoying the nature around her. Gabboons still came to stay with her, and she continued to guide their research. Another great

ILLUSTRATION BY FRANCES HAMERSTROM, HAMERSTROM FAMILY ARCHIVES

horned owl named Porfirio kept her company. As she neared the end of her life, her children and grandchildren, friends, and former gabboons all visited her.

Fran's drawing of a male prairie chicken

In 1998, at the age of 90, Fran Hamerstrom died of cancer. Friends said she kept her spirit and independence until the end.

Dubai (doo **bı**): a city and territory in the country of the United Arab Emirates   **sheik** (sheek): an Arab chief, ruler, or prince   **Peru** (puh **roo**): a country in western South America

In 1996, both Fran and Frederick were inducted into the Wisconsin Conservation Hall of Fame in Stevens Point, Wisconsin. The Hamerstroms' memorial at the Hall of Fame reads, "They leave the world a better place than they found it."

What **legacy** did the Hamerstroms leave to the people of Wisconsin? They were among the first conservationists to prove the connection between habitat and survival of a species. They followed Aldo Leopold's method of researching wildlife in their natural habitats. Their 30-year study of the prairie chicken was a model for wildlife research for scientists all over the country. They assembled a tremendous body of research for future **ornithologists** to build on.

Even more importantly, the Hamerstroms inspired many future scientists to follow in their footsteps. When Fran and Frederick first began working in the field of wildlife management, they had few environmental role models. Their dedication to wildlife rubbed off on others.

Former gabboon Ron Sauey and close friend George Archibald founded the International Crane Foundation in

legacy (**leg** uh see): something that is handed down from one generation to another
ornithologist (or nuh **thah** luh jist): a scientist who studies birds

Baraboo, Wisconsin. Gabboon Keith Bildstein became a researcher at Hawk Mountain, a raptor refuge in Pennsylvania. Peter Kramer, the son of their lifelong friend, Gustave Kramer, became a leader with the World Wildlife Federation.

"They infected a whole generation of young workers with the same enthusiasm, the same devotion, and the same feeling of doing what makes life worthwhile," said Ernst Mayr, the Hamerstroms' friend and fellow scientist.

International Crane Foundation

In 1973, Ron Sauey and George Archibald founded the International Crane Foundation in Baraboo, Wisconsin. Both men loved cranes and were determined to save them from extinction.

Fifteen species of cranes live around the world. Many of them are endangered. Crane populations are declining because of loss of habitat. Cranes need a wetland and grassland habitat to survive. The International Crane Foundation works with people all over the world to preserve wetland and grassland habitats in order to save the cranes.

The United States has only 2 native crane species: the sandhill crane and the whooping crane. The whooping crane is endangered.

But the International Crane Foundation is committed to saving it.

In the 1940s only 22 whooping cranes lived in North America. Today, there are almost 600. The International Crane Foundation helps **captive** whooping cranes breed and hatch their eggs. Scientists also research ways to successfully release the young cranes into the wild.

Wetlands habitat helps cranes and other birds survive in the wild.

The Crane Foundation is the only place in the world where you can see all 15 species of cranes in one place. Captive cranes of each species are bred at the Foundation to increase the population of some of the endangered birds. The captive cranes produce more than 100 crane eggs each season. Some of these chicks are raised and released in the wild. Others are kept to hatch future chicks. Ron Sauey and George Archibald both believed that breeding birds in captivity could save them from extinction. Without the work of the International Crane Foundation, another species could be lost forever.

captive: confined to a place and not able to escape

101

Fran and Frederick did a lot in their lifetimes. In Wisconsin they are remembered most for saving the greater prairie chicken from extinction. But the battle to save the prairie chicken is not over.

Wisconsin's prairie chickens are threatened once again. Today, scientists estimate the prairie chicken population in central Wisconsin to be between 600 and 800 birds. That is less than half of the population that Fran and Frederick studied in the 1950s. If the prairie chicken population gets much smaller, there may not be enough birds to breed and reproduce successfully.

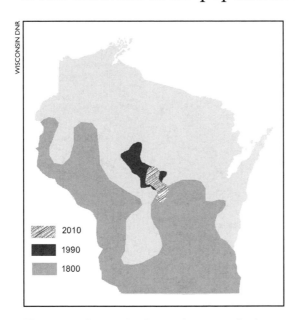

WISCONSIN DNR

2010
1990
1800

This map shows the loss of prairie chicken habitat in Wisconsin.

Scientists believe the survival of the prairie chickens depends on expanding their grassland habitat. Grasslands available for prairie chickens have steadily decreased over the last 20 years.

The small group of prairie chickens on the grasslands in central Wisconsin has become isolated from other flocks of prairie chickens. This makes them **genetically** weaker and unhealthier. A disease or weather **catastrophe** could quickly kill the flock.

Prairie chickens from other states have been brought in and bred with the prairie chickens in central Wisconsin. But this is only a temporary solution. Conservation groups estimate that 15,000 more acres of grassland will be needed to support growth of a healthy prairie chicken population. New grasslands should be connected to other nearby wildlife areas. Prairie chickens from those areas would help produce a stronger, healthier population. If we want to continue to have prairie chickens in Wisconsin, we will have to work even harder to save their habitat.

genetically (juh **ne** ti klee): relating to genes, which control the development of traits passed from parent to offspring   **catastrophe** (kuh **tas** truh fee): a sudden disaster

Fran and Frederick's daughter Elva painted this view of prairie chickens on the Buena Vista booming grounds.

Thanks to the efforts of wildlife pioneers like the Hamerstroms, we know that loss of habitat means loss of wildlife. As the world's population grows, animals continue to lose their habitat. More of them will become endangered and extinct. Remember that we share the world with birds, animals, and insects that are helpful to us and bring us joy. Our actions can encourage their survival.

Fran and Frederick Hamerstrom believed it was possible to live together with the animals around them. They modeled this belief throughout their entire life. What can you do to continue their fight?

Appendix

Fran and Frederick's Time Line

1907 — Fran is born on December 17, in Boston, Massachusetts.

1909 — Frederick is born on July 8, in Trenton, New Jersey.

1912–1914 — Fran's family lives in Dresden, Germany.

1928 — Fran meets Frederick on a blind date at Dartmouth College.

1931 — Fran and Frederick secretly marry on February 18 in Deland, Florida. They have a formal ceremony in Massachusetts in June.

Fran and Frederick begin school at the Game Conservation Institute in Clinton, New Jersey.

Frederick hears Aldo Leopold speak about a new career called wildlife management.

1932 — Frederick and Fran move to Ames, Iowa, where Frederick begins a job as a wildlife research assistant to Dr. Paul Errington. Both Fran and Frederick return to college.

1935 — Fran graduates from Iowa State College. Frederick receives his master's degree in zoology from Iowa State College.

Fran and Frederick move to Necedah, Wisconsin, where Frederick works for the Resettlement Administration.

1937 — Fran and Frederick move to Madison, Wisconsin, to study wildlife management under Aldo Leopold. Frederick pursues a PhD and Fran a master's degree.

1938 — In December, Fran and Frederick move to Hancock, Wisconsin. Frederick begins a graduate research project on prairie chickens. Fran's graduate project is on chickadees.

1940 — Fran receives her master's degree as the only female graduate student of Aldo Leopold.

Alan Hamerstrom is born on November 9 in Madison, Wisconsin.

1941 — Frederick receives his PhD from the University of Wisconsin. The Hamerstroms move to Pinckney, Michigan, where Frederick works as curator of the Edwin S. George Reserve at the University of Michigan at Ann Arbor.

1943 — Elva Hamerstrom is born on March 25 in Ann Arbor, Michigan. Frederick enlists in World War II.

1945 — Frederick is discharged from the army, and the Hamerstroms move back to Michigan.

1946–1948 — The Hamerstroms are involved in "The Action," a movement to save European scientists and their families from starvation after World War II.

1949 — The Hamerstroms move back to Plainfield, Wisconsin, to work for the Wisconsin Conservation Department.

1971 — The Hamerstroms receive the National Wildlife Federation's Distinguished Service Award for Wildlife Conservation.

1972 — The Hamerstroms retire from the Wisconsin Department of Natural Resources.

1990 — Frederick dies of cancer on March 28.

1996 — Fran and Frederick Hamerstrom are both inducted into the Wisconsin Conservation Hall of Fame.

1998 — Fran dies on August 29 in Port Edwards, Wisconsin.

Glossary

Pronunciation Key

a	cat (kat), plaid (plad), half (haf)		**oh**	open (**oh** puhn), sew (soh)
			oi	boil (boil), boy (boi)
ah	father (**fah** THUr), heart (hahrt)		**oo**	pool (pool), move (moov), shoe (shoo)
air	carry (**kair** ee), bear (bair), where (whair)		**or**	order (**or** dur), more (mor)
aw	all (awl), law (law), bought (bawt)		**ou**	house (hous), now (nou)
			u	good (gud), should (shud)
ay	say (say), break (brayk), vein (vayn)		**uh**	cup (kuhp), flood (fluhd), button (**buht** uhn)
e	bet (bet), says (sez), deaf (def)		**ur**	burn (burn), pearl (purl), bird (burd)
ee	bee (bee), team (teem), fear (feer)		**yoo**	use (yooz), few (fyoo), view (vyoo)
i	bit (bit), women (**wim** uhn), build (bild)		**hw**	what (hwuht), when (hwen)
I	ice (Is), lie (lI), sky (skI)		**TH**	that (THat), breathe (breeTH)
o	hot (hot), watch (wotch)		**zh**	measure (**mezh** ur), garage (guh **razh**)

108

abundant (uh **buhn** duhnt): present in large numbers

binocular (buh **nah** kyuh lur): hand-held instrument used for seeing at a distance

booming season: the time of year, usually late March through April, when male prairie chickens perform their displays in hopes of attracting females

breed: produce or increase animals or plants by sexual reproduction

capital punishment: the legally authorized killing of someone as punishment for a crime

captive: confined to a place and not able to escape

catastrophe (kuh **tas** truh fee): a sudden disaster

century (**sen** chuh ree): a period of 100 years

circulated (**sur** kyuh lay tid): passed from place to place or from person to person

conviction (kuhn **vik** shuhn): a strong belief or opinion

criminologist (krim uh **nah** luh jist): someone who studies crime, criminals, and the punishment of criminals

curator (**kyoor** ay tur): a person in charge of a museum or zoo

crusade: campaign to get things changed for the better

degree: title given to students by a college or university

depleted (di **plee** tid): reduced by using up

devastating (**dev** uh stay ting): destroying entirely or nearly entirely

dominant (**dom** uh nuhnt): controlling or being more powerful or important than all others

Dubai (doo **bī**): a city and territory in the country of the United Arab Emirates

ecology (ee **kah** luh jee): a branch of science concerned with the relationships between living things and their environment

ecosystem (**ee** koh sis tuhm): the whole group of living and nonliving things that make up an environment and affect each other

editing: preparation of written material for publication by correcting or modifying it

embroidery (im **broi** dur ee): needlework done to decorate cloth

estimated (**es** tuh may tuhd): gave or formed a general idea of the value, size, or cost of something

ethic: a rule of moral behavior governing an individual or group

excess (**ek** ses): too much

extinction (ek **sting** shuhn): no longer existing or being alive

foreign (**for** uhn): belonging to another place or country

game: an animal hunted for sport or for food

genetically (juh **ne** ti klee): relating to genes, which control the development of traits passed from parent to offspring

governess: a woman who teaches and trains a child especially in a private home

graduate program: a school, usually at a university that offers degrees beyond the bachelor's degree

Great Depression: a time from October 29, 1929, into the 1930s when businesses did badly and many people became poor

grouse (grous): a brownish bird, mostly in wooded areas, that feeds especially on the ground and is sometimes hunted for food or sport

habitat: the place where a plant or animal grows or lives in nature

habitation (ha buh **tay** shuhn): the act of living in a place

hospitality (hahs puh **tal** uh tee): friendly and generous treatment of guests

impending (im **pen** ding): happening or likely to happen soon

irrigation (ir uh **gay** shuhn): supplying with water

jesses: short straps secured on the leg of a bird, usually with a ring for attaching a leash

kestrel: (**kes** truhl) small falcon that hovers in the air while searching for prey

lard: soft white fat sometimes used for cooking

legacy (**leg** uh see): something that is handed down from one generation to another

legendary (**le** juhn der ee): very famous

lulled: made sleepy

majored: specialized in a particular subject at a college or university

marsh: an area of soft wet land with grasses and related plants

mentor: someone who teaches or gives help and advice to a less experienced and often younger person

naturalist (**na** chuh ruh list): person who studies nature and especially plants and animals as they live in nature

nylons (**nı** lahnz): stockings

ornithologist (or nuh **thah** luh jist): a scientist who studies birds

ornithology (or nuh **thah** luh jee): a branch of science that deals with the study of birds

pellets: wads of material (like bone and fur) that cannot be digested and has been thrown up by a bird of prey

Peru (puh **roo**): a country in western South America

phalanx (**fay** langks): a large group of people, animals, or things often placed close together

PhD: the highest degree given by a graduate program

Pilgrims: English colonists who founded the first permanent settlement in New England in 1620

plumage (**ploo** mij): the feathers of a bird

plumbing (**pluh** ming): system of pipes and fixtures for supplying and carrying off water in a building

pollywog (**pah** lee wahg): a tadpole, or the larva of a frog or toad that has a long tail, breathes with gills, and lives in water

poverty (**pov** ur tee): the condition of being poor

Pygmies (**pig** meez): members of a group of very small people who live in Africa

raptors: birds that kill and eat other animals for food

reassure (ree uh **shur**): to make someone feel less afraid, upset, or doubtful

rebellious (ruh **bel** yuhs): fighting against or refusing to obey authority

rehabilitator (ree uh **bil** uh tay tur): a person who helps to bring someone or something back to a normal, healthy condition after an illness or injury

reputation (rep yoo **tay** shuhn): overall quality or character as judged by people in general

rudder: a movable flat piece attached at the rear of a ship or aircraft for steering

sheik (sheek): an Arab chief, ruler, or prince

species (**spee** seez): a group of similar plants or animals

spectacular (spek **ta** kyuh lur): striking

squeamish (**skwee** mish): hesitant because of shock or disgust

stopover: stop made during a journey

strove: tried very hard

subspecies (**suhb** spee seez): a group of related plants or animals that is smaller than a species

supervised (**soo** pur vizd): coordinated and directed the activities of

Swahili (swah **hee** lee): a language widely used in East Africa and the Congo region

tamarack (**tam** uh rak): a type of tree that is related to the pines and that drops its needles in the winter

technique (tek **neek**): a way of doing something using special knowledge or skill

territory: area that is occupied and defended by an animal or group of animals

theses (**thee** seez): essays presenting results of original research

thrived (thrīvd): grew or developed very well

tradition: belief or custom handed down from one generation to another

transferred (**trans** furd): moved from one place to another

tympani (**tim** puh nee): one of a set of 2 or 3 large drums that are played by one performer in an orchestra

underdog: a person or team thought to have little chance of winning

unique (yoo **neek**): being the only one of its kind

victorious (vik **tor** ee uhs): having won a victory

vivid (**vi** vuhd): very strong or bright

whetted (**hwet** id): made stronger

Zaire (zah **ir**): a Central African state, now known as the Democratic Republic of the Congo

zoology (zoh **ah** luh jee): a branch of biology concerned with the study of animals and animal life

Reading Group Guide and Activities

Discussion Questions

❖ Though Fran and Frederick worked side by side throughout their lives, Fran often worked for no pay or was paid less than Frederick. Why do you think that was? Do men and women earn the same amount today? Why or why not? How could you find out? Why did Fran have to prove she was just as smart and capable as a man? How did she do it?

❖ How did Fran's childhood differ from your own? When would you rather have been born, then or now? How would your life be different?

❖ The Hamerstroms were pioneers in the brand-new science of ecology. How did they pass on their beliefs and knowledge to a new generation? Think of your own family. What beliefs or knowledge have you learned from your parents? What will you pass down to future generations?

❖ The Hamerstroms worked together as a team throughout their whole lives. Yet they had very different personalities. Name some qualities they each had that made them successful partners. Do you think being different helped them work together or made it harder? Why?

❖ Aldo Leopold once said, "Wild things were taken for granted until progress began to do away with them. Now we face the question whether a still higher 'standard of living' is worth its cost in things natural, wild, and free." What did Leopold mean by this statement? Do you agree or disagree with him? Why?

Activities

❧ Aldo Leopold's "land ethic" belief was that we are happier when we live in harmony with the natural areas around us. Think of the things in nature that you value the most. Create an inspirational poster using the word NATURE and a phrase summarizing your beliefs.

❧ Pick an endangered species from the Environmental Education for Kids website: http://dnr.wi.gov/org/caer/ce/eek/earth/endangered .htm. Create a flyer with information about the species. Include information on why it is endangered and a plan to help it recover.

❧ Pick another member of the Wisconsin Conservation Hall of Fame from the following website: www.wchf.org/. Using a computer or by hand, print/draw their picture and make an award certificate that explains why they were inducted into the Hall of Fame.

❧ For one week, keep a log of all the birds you see outside your window. Choose one of the birds. Research and write a paragraph about the habitat that bird needs in order to thrive. Include information on what it eats and where it likes to nest. Draw or take a picture of as many of the birds that you can and include them in your log. Describe what you can do to help birds thrive in your neighborhood.

❧ As a boy, Aldo Leopold kept a nature journal in which he recorded all the animals and birds he saw around his house. Keep a nature journal for a week. Write observations of what is happening around you in nature. What do you see? What do you discover? Don't forget to draw the world around you!

To Learn More about Prairie Chickens and Other Endangered Species

Central Wisconsin Prairie Chicken Festival:
www.prairiechickenfestival.org

Central Wisconsin Kestrel Project: www.kestrelresearch.com

Environmental Education for Kids:
dnr.wi.gov/org/caer/ce/eek/critter/bird/prairiechicken.htm

International Crane Foundation: www.savingcranes.org

Necedah National Wildlife Refuge:
www.fws.gov/refuge/Necedah/about.html

Society of Tympanuchus Cupidus Pinnatus:
www.prairiegrouse.org/STCP.html

University of Wisconsin–Stevens Point, Wisconsin's Prairie Chickens:
http://www.uwsp.edu/wildlife/pchicken/Pages/default.aspx

Wisconsin Raptor Education Group: www.raptoreducationgroup.org

Wisconsin Conservation Hall of Fame: www.wchf.org

Acknowledgments

One of my greatest pleasures in writing this book was hearing the many stories of Fran and Frederick from their friends and acquaintances throughout central Wisconsin. The stories poured out, often beginning, "I was a gabboon one summer . . ." or "I remember their red VW van on campus . . ." It soon became obvious that Fran and Frederick left their mark on the area.

I must especially thank Elva Hamerstrom Paulson, who patiently filled in the gaps in my research with fascinating stories of growing up in the Hamerstrom household. Her wry sense of humor and attention to detail helped my understanding of her family more than any other reference source. Elva enthusiastically combed through family photos to include in the book and even offered her own wildlife drawings that add so much to the flavor of the Hamerstrom story.

Mary Casey Martin, Fran's literary gabboon, was also encouraging and helpful in clarifying many of the different stories I heard about the Hamerstroms.

Several teachers, school staff, and friends read through the manuscript and helped with ideas to improve it. These special people include Cindy Byers, Janet Eschenbauch, Becky Sturdy, Karen Dostal, Cyndy Irvine, and Jane Van Haren.

Lesa Kardash, from the Department of Natural Resources, and Dan O'Connell, from the Portage County Land Conservation Department, helped me with much of the information about prairie chicken research and the Buena Vista marsh. Sharon Schwab, from the Central Wisconsin Grassland Conservation Area Partnership, provided photos and additional prairie chicken information. Dr. Christine Thomas, from the College of Natural Resources at the University of Wisconsin–Stevens Point, lent me her file of Hamerstrom newspaper clippings.

Finally, thanks to my husband, Jim McKnight, for reading the manuscript, providing helpful ideas and encouragement, and braving a bitter cold April morning to view the unforgettable prairie chicken dance with me.

Index

This index points you to the pages where you can read about persons, places, and ideas. If you do not find the word you are looking for, try to think of another word that means about the same thing.

When you see a page number in **bold** it means there is a picture on that page.

A

"The Action" (German relief effort), 59–60
Aldo Leopold Foundation, 27
Ambrose (great horned owl), **88**, 88–89
Anweiler, Gary, **92**
Archibald, George, 99–100

B

Bildstein, Keith, 100
bird "aging," 55
bird banding, 53–54, 68–69, **69**, 85
bird blinds, 54, **54**
bird breeding, 87
Bird Man, 29
bluegrass, 76, 82
boomers (volunteer helpers), 70–73
booming season, 2, 50–51, 69–74, **104**
Buena Vista Grasslands, 1, 54, **76**, 76–77, **81**, 81–82, **104**
Bug Woman, 29

C

Central Wisconsin Game Project, 38–39, **39**
Central Wisconsin Kestrel Research, 90
chemicals, banned, 89–90
"the chicken people," 79
Chrys (golden eagle), 87
conservation partners, 76–77
conservation principles, 26–27
Cooperative Wildlife Research Unit, 27
cranes, 40–41, 99–101

D

Dane County Conservation League, 78
Darrow, Clarence, 19–20, **20**
DDT (chemical), 89–90
De La Rhonde, Deann, 97
Department of Natural Resources (DNR), 41, 65, 78, 82
Distinguished Service Award for Wildlife Conservation, 94
dust storm of 1934, 33–34

E

eagles, 84, **84**, 87
ecologists, role of, 3–4
endangered species
    gray wolf, 40
    Karner blue butterfly, 40
    prairie chickens, 48, **48**, 49, 102
    sandhill cranes, 40
    whooping cranes, 41, **41**, 100–101
Errington, Paul, 27, 29
extinctions
    heath hens, 12–13, 51
    passenger pigeons, **36**, 36–38, **38**
    prairie chickens, 49, 75, 102
    uncontrolled hunting and, 25, 27,
    35–36, 48
    whooping cranes, 41, 100–101

F

falconry, 83–84
farmer–conservationist relationship,
31–32, 79, 80
field study projects, 28–29, 42, 46–47,
70–74, **73**, 88–90
Frauta (German Governess), 8, 11

G

gabboons (research volunteers), 90–93,
92, 98, 99–100
Game Conservation Institute, 23–25
German relief effort, 59–60
Gila National Wilderness, 27
grasslands, 1, 54, 74, 76, **76**, 81–82, **104**
gray wolf, 40
Great Central Wisconsin Swamp, 40–41

Great Depression, 31–32, 38
great horned owls, 88, **88**, 98
greater prairie chicken, 50
grouse family, 50, 65

H

habitat, 3–4, 48, 74, **102**, 102–103
Hamerstrom, Alan (son), 57, **58**, 60–62
Hamerstrom, Elva (daughter), 57, **58**,
60–63, **62**, 104
Hamerstrom, Frances (Fran), **6**, **7**, **15**, **23**,
24, **47**, **58**, **84**
    bird "aging," 55
    Bug Woman, 29
    childhood, 6–14
    childhood home, 8–10, **9**
    controversial lifestyle, 79–80
    cooking reputation, 63
    death, 98
    Distinguished Service Award for
    Wildlife Conservation, 94
    education, 15, 23–25, 27, 29–30, 56, 58
    at Game Conservation Institute, 23–25
    German relief effort, 59–60
    insect collections, 11, 29
    interest in raptors, 13–14
    life in Germany, 8
    marriage to Frederick, 21–22, **23**
    modeling career, 15
    parenting style, 61–62
    passion for nature, 9–10
    passion for raptors, 83–87
    passion for wildlife, 2–5
    pet kestrel, 13–14
    rebellious teen years, 14–15
    retirement years, 94–98

121

secret garden, 10
and traditional roles for women, 7, 23, 42, 56, 79–80, 84, 95–96
writing career, 43
Hamerstrom, Frederick Jr., **16**, **19**, **23**, **24**, **47**, **58**, **95**
bird and mammal collection, 29
Bird Man, 29
childhood, 16–18
death, 97
Distinguished Service Award for Wildlife Conservation, 94
education, 18–19, 27, 29–30, 56, 58
at Game Conservation Institute, 23–25
German relief effort, 59–60
high school years, 17–19
influenced by Clarence Darrow, 19–20
marriage to Fran, 21–22, **23**
nicknamed Hammy, 16
odd jobs, 18
parenting style, 61–62
passion for nature, 19
passion for wildlife, 2–5
reputation for honesty and hard work, 18
during World War II, 59
Hamerstrom, Frederick Sr. (father), **17**
Hamerstrom, Helen Davis (mother), **17**
Hamerstrom family
children, 57, **58**, 60–63, **62**, 104
homes, **32**, 43–44, **67**, 67–68, **68**, 70–71
leisure, 61, 63–64
lifestyle, 67–68, 79–80, 96
parenting styles, 61–62
pets, 13–14, 61–63, **62**, 84, 87–89, **88**

Hamerstrom legacy, 99–100
harriers (marsh hawks), 88
Hawk Mountain, 100
heath hens, 12–13, 51
hunting, 24, 26–27, 35–37, 48

I
insect and butterfly collection, **12**
International Crane Foundation, 41, 99–101
irrigation systems, 75

J
jack pines, 34, **34**
jesses, 13

K
Karner blue butterfly, 40
kestrels, 13–14, 88, 90
Kramer, Peter, 100

L
land management, 33–34, **34**, 75, 78–79. *See also* scatter land management plan
Leopold, Aldo, **3**, **26**, **47**
conservation principles, 26–27
death, 65
the "father of ecology," 3
friendship with Hamerstroms, 30
passenger pigeon speech, 37–38
as teacher, 46–48
UW game management program, 45
and wildlife management, 25, 26

M

Mayr, Ernst, 100
Minerva (pet owl), 61, **62**
Muir, John, 36

N

Nancy (golden eagle), 87
national wilderness areas, 27
National Wildlife Federation, 94
Necedah family home, **32**, 43-44
Necedah National Wildlife Refuge, 35,
39, 40-41
North American Falconers Association,
83, 84

O

observation sheets, **73**
overhunting, 32
owl pellets, 28, **29**
owls, 28, **88**, 88-89, **92**, 98

P

passenger pigeons, **36**, 36-38, **38**
Pilgrims, 51
Plainfield family home, **67**, 67-68, **68**,
70-71
Porfirio (great horned owl), 98
prairie chickens, **2**, **4**, **48**, **50**, **66**, **72**, **98**,
104
    booming season, 2, 50-51, 69-74
    data collection, 70-74, **73**
    endangered status, 1-2
    food and nesting material, 76, 82

habitat, 3-4, 48, 74, 80-81, **81**, **102**,
102-103
    species decline, 48-55, 66

R

raptor rehabilitation, 86-87
raptors, 83-87, **84**
research projects, 28-29, 42, 46-47,
70-74, **73**, 88-90
Resettlement Administration, 34-35, 45
resource conservation, 35-36
roadkill, 91
Rockford Bunch, 84-85
ruffed grouse, 50

S

A Sand County Almanac (Leopold), 26
sandhill cranes, 40, 100
Sauey, Ron, 99-100
scatter land management plan, 75-79,
77, 80, 82
Seri community (Mexico), 94-95
sharp-tailed grouse, 50
Society of Tympanuchus Cupido
Pinnatus, 78
soil conservation, 34
spruce grouse, 50

T

Thomas, Christine, 92
traps and trap lines, 51-53, **52**
Tympanuchus cupido pinnatus (prairie
chicken), 50

W

waterfowl habitat, 40

wetland bogs, 40

whooping cranes, 41, **41**, 100-101

wilderness areas, national, 27

The Wilderness Society, 27

wildlife management, 25, 45

wildlife refuges, 35-36

Wisconsin

    DDT (chemical) ban, 89-90

    Department of Natural Resources (DNR), 41, 65, 78, 82

    Dust Bowl, **33**, 33-34

    endangered species, 102

    farming, 31-32

    Great Depression in, 31-32

    land management, 33-34, **34**, 75, 78-79

    wetland bogs, 40

    wild game supply, 32

Wisconsin Conservation Department, 65, 76

Wisconsin Conservation Hall of Fame, 99

Wisconsin Conservation League, 78

Wisconsin Department of Natural Resources, 41, 65, 78, 82

Wisconsin Society for Ornithology, 78

women, traditional roles for, 7, 23, 42, 56, 79-80, 84, 95-96

World War II, 59-60